J. KRISHNAMURTI
AS I KNEW HIM

J. Krishnamurti
As I Knew Him

Susunaga Weeraperuma

MOTILAL BANARSIDASS PUBLISHERS
PRIVATE LIMITED • DELHI

First Edition: Bombay, 1988
Second Revised Edition: Delhi, 1996

ISBN: 81-208-1427-4

Also available at:

MOTILAL BANARSIDASS
41 U.A. Bungalow Road, Jawahar Nagar, Delhi 110 007
8 Mahalaxmi Chamber, Warden Road, Mumbai 400 026
120 Royapettah High Road, Mylapore, Madras 600 004
Sanas Plaza, Subhash Nagar, Pune 411 002
16 St. Mark's Road, Bangalore 560 001
8 Camac Street, Calcutta 700 017
Ashok Rajpath, Patna 800 004
Chowk, Varanasi 221 001

PRINTED IN INDIA
BY JAINENDRA PRAKASH JAIN AT SHRI JAINENDRA PRESS,
A-45 NARAINA, PHASE I, NEW DELHI 110 028
AND PUBLISHED BY NARENDRA PRAKASH JAIN FOR
MOTILAL BANARSIDASS PUBLISHERS PRIVATE LIMITED,
BUNGALOW ROAD, DELHI 110 007

This book is lovingly dedicated

to

CLAUDIA

Preface

I was closely associated with Sri J. Krishnamurti and enthusiastically involved in his work for some 30 years.

Most of the passages in this book are taken from my notebooks. Unfortunately I have never been able to bring myself to keeping a diary but I have written long accounts of my many interesting private meetings and interviews with Krishnaji and other outstanding personalities.

This work is not a biography of Krishnaji, although, as may be expected, it abounds in biographical information as well as his observations on questions of great spiritual interest.

The anecdotes of Krishnaji's life given here have a certain deep and hidden philosophical meaning. Anecdotes assist us to understand his enigmatic personality. Even his jokes and casual remarks should be taken seriously because they apparently emanated from that creative inward silence which he termed 'the otherness'.

Susunaga Weeraperuma

CONTENTS

Dialogues between Krishnamurti and the Author

The Abode of Enlightenment

As a schoolboy I used to spend my afternoons and evenings in the Colombo Public Library. There some of the happiest days of my life were spent. There I would lose myself in the mysteriously enchanting world of thousands of books, magazines and newspapers from different countries. It seemed a far more interesting way of spending one's leisure hours than wasting it on silly games, sports or athletics. One day while browsing the shelves for something new to read I came across a slim volume called *The Path.* Its frontispiece consisted of a black and white photograph of a fine portrait head by Antoine Bourdelle. For a few minutes I was enraptured by the sheer beauty of this masterpiece of sculpture. All the features of the face harmoniously blended. As a lover of beauty I could not remain unmoved by the subtle magnetism and nobility of the face. At first I thought that this was a piece of classical Greek sculpture but later found that it was no other than the head of J. Krishnamurti. That was how I discovered Krishnaji whose teachings have been the most important and formative influence in my life. It was this purely aesthetic reaction to his outward appearance that initially drew me to the teachings.

Many years later it was a joyful experience to visit the Musee Bourdelle in Paris where I saw the original of the above-mentioned portrait head. Bourdelle sculptured several portrait heads of Krishnamurti which are on permanent display in this museum. It is noteworthy that this great sculptor held Krishnamurti in high esteem. Bourdelle maintained that for Krishnamurti "the eternal things are the only things which matter."

Given my Buddhist upbringing, I naturally found *The Path* (1924) totally absorbing. This long essay is a poetic description of Krishnamurti's struggles and pains in his search for illumination. I felt that this book was portraying the sorrow of samsara with its cycle of births and deaths and the freedom therefrom. The gist of this work is contained in the following sentence: "Come all ye that sorrow, and enter with me into the abode of enlightenment and into the shades of immortality."

What is there in a Name?

For numerous persons the name "Krishnamurti" is synonymous with "Enlightenment". "Krishnamurti" means "in the likeness of God." The name was well chosen. Unlike so many snobbish persons, Krishnamurti was not attached to his name and never gave it importance. A name is only a label and a means of identification. Often K referred to himself as "the speaker" or simply "K". Henceforth I shall also call him "K" instead of using his long name, although I realise that "K" is no substitute for

"Krishnaji" which was the respectful and affectionate name we always used when addressing him.

No name can adequately describe the man who represented that which is nameless.

First Impressions of Krishnamurti

I was very young when for the first time I saw K in the flesh on Christmas day in 1949. Those reminiscences have already been described in my book *Living and Dying from Moment to Moment* (Bombay : Chetana, 1978):

> "I first became interested in Krishnamurti during my schoolboy days in 1949 and heard him for the first time in Colombo that year. I still vividly remember standing in a huge crowd who were impatiently awaiting the arrival of a certain holy man called Krishnamurti at the Town Hall of Colombo. At last the mayoral car arrived and there he was, a slim figure seated nervously by the side of the then mayor, the late Dr. Kumaran Rutnam, a well-known local Communist politician. Krishnamurti still had black hair with streaks of grey around the temples. He darted from the limousine and ran up the flight of steps in an attempt to avoid the prying eyes of the hundreds of devotees. He was elegantly dressed in a white silk dhoti. That first impression of him has never faded from my memory, particularly because as a child I was not accustomed to seeing holy men so opulently dressed. I had been conditioned by the example of Mahatma Gandhi who only wore a loin cloth."

During the subsequent public meetings there were better opportunities to observe him more closely.

Those mellow and faraway eyes of his were a surprise because I had expected to find in him the peculiarly fiery and luminous eyes of a yogi. For at that time I had seen several outstanding Indian yogis, including Swami Sivananda who had invited me to stay in his Rishikesh ashram in the Himalayas. Luminous eyes are generally associated with intellectual brilliance whereas mellow eyes signify serenity and compassion.

Monkish Objection

I used to study Buddhism at the Vajirarama Temple in Colombo. One of the bhikkus (Buddhist monks) of this monastery tried his best to dissuade me from attending K's talks. He said: "Nobody can surpass the Buddha. This man Krishnamurti is merely preaching a refined kind of Buddhism."

I responded : "If it is refined Buddhism then why are you so opposed to it?"

An Arhat?

This monk murmured against K after attending a discussion meeting: "Why is Krishnamurti so excitable? If he is an arhat should he not always be calm?" I said : "Venerable sir, the difficulty is that you have a concept about how an arhat should behave. Have you ever really met an arhat? As I understand it, an arhat is not devoid of thoughts and feelings. Strong emotions are inevitable in any intelligent and sensitive person. Although an arhat will naturally experience thoughts and feelings none of these ever gets permanently established in his mind. An arhat is free only in the sense that he has no substratum of thoughts and feelings — no background."

Dignified Composure

At one of the discussion meetings a prominent politician was present. He made insulting and abusive remarks and even went to the extent of calling K an impostor. K remained tranquil and continued with the discussion as though nothing had happened. On another occasion a man scolded K and used foul language. K responded : "What is your problem, Sir?"

This man soon became the laughing-stock of the audience because it was obvious that he had resorted to using grossly offensive words only because he was deeply agitated within himself. Over the years something I repeatedly observed about K was that he was neither flattered by praise nor hurt by criticisms and insults. K was like a mighty tree that always remained unruffled in a storm. Weaker. trees wildly swayed in the wind but the mighty tree never lost its dignified composure even under the most trying circumstances.

University of Ceylon

The students of the University of Ceylon (as it was then called) in Colombo behaved in a shockingly hostile manner when K was invited to address them. All the seats of the hall were occupied which was not surprising because celebrities usually attracted large crowds. In this hall I have often seen students jeering at famous statesmen, eminent politicians and men of letters. I suppose that is their crude way of showing their defiance of authority; probably some were giving vent to their pent-up frustration, aggression and violence.

K met with a mixed reception as he entered the

hall. Some clapped their hands and applauded but many unashamedly booed him. His speech was repeatedly interrupted. K was heckled several times. Then K asked why they were behaving like that because he was after all their guest speaker who had been specially invited to give them a talk. K continued to talk despite the disturbances and there was not even a hint of resentment in his attitude to the students. At times he actually joined the students in their laughter. He delivered a particularly eloquent and moving address. Some of the students who had earlier behaved in an unruly manner later apologised to him.

I do not actually remember hearing the student-chairman paying K the following compliment but I am relying on G. Venkatachalam's report of this memorable meeting in his book *My Contemporaries*. The student-chairman of the meeting had earlier denounced K but later, at the end of the meeting, he went to the extent of praising him as the modern Socrates and the greatest teacher after the Buddha.

Jawaharlal Nehru

K's visit to Colombo coincided with the Commonwealth Prime Ministers' Conference in that city. Famous statesmen like Pandit Jawaharlal Nehru and Ernest Bevin were in Colombo with the result that the newspapers were unfortunately devoting too much space to reporting the activities of these statesmen and therefore insufficiently publicizing the presence of K in our midst. Persons seriously interested in the teachings of K were understandably upset that politicians and statesmen had overshadowed K. Then a leading newspaper reported an incident which subtly redressed this imbalance of publicity.

Pandit Nehru was a state guest and he resided at Queen's House, the palatial mansion of the Governor-General. One morning the security guards were panic-stricken because the Indian Prime Minister was missing. No one had a clue as to his whereabouts. Had he been kidnapped? Then suddenly Pandit Nehru appeared on the scene in a car. The explanation given for his disappearance is interesting. After hearing that K was in town, Nehru decided to visit the sage secretly and privately and pay his respects.

The Immense Sky

There is a lovely lake in the vicinity of Slave Island, a busy suburb of Colombo. The time of day that K particularly liked for walking by this lake was the hour immediately following sunset when it is cool and nice. Sometimes he walked so fast by the narrow footpath surrounding the lake that one feared the possibility of his tripping over a stone and falling into the muddy waters that abound in water-snakes. This was not a groundless fear but a reasonable one, especially because one evening he was walking in a trance of ecstasy with his head held high. He was continuously gazing at the scarlet sky and seemed quite oblivious to the narrow footpath and the adjoining lake. An accident seemed imminent. Then my friend jumped forward to protect K. K immediately held his hand and said : "Sir, look at the sky. The sky opens the mind." We returned home and pondered whether to take K's remark seriously. Was he suggesting that sky-gazing is a mind-expanding activity? But had not

K spoken against the practice of techniques to bring about awareness? We discussed the question thoroughly but unfortunately we were left in a state of confusion.

Several years later I met this friend and we recalled this incident by the lake. He stated that he often looked at the heavens and enjoyed doing so; he also mentioned that he did not observe the skies, as the astronomers do, with a special purpose in mind. We both agreed that important though it is to watch the sky, mountains and seas and thus commune with nature, nevertheless such communing should never be regarded as a spiritual practice or sadhana. An alert and sensitive individual cannot help communing with nature; it is a pure action that has no underlying motive, something that is done for its own sake.

Dr. E.W. Adikaram

It is necessary to write at length about the life and activities of Adikaram, who was one of K's closest friends and admirers. When I was a teenager, my attitude to the personality and teachings of K was largely influenced by the views of this remarkable philosopher called Adikaram.

Eminent Sri Lankan educationist, prolific writer, Pali scholar, and author of scientific books in Sinhalese, Adikaram obtained his Doctorate in Philosophy from the University of London for a thesis titled *Early History of Buddhism in Ceylon or State of Buddhism in Ceylon as Revealed by the Pali Commentaries of the 5th Century A.D.* He had been a Theosophist and a follower of Mahatma Gandhi, but the predominant formative factor in his life was the teaching of K. His controversial books and articles with their Krishnamurtiesque interpretation of Buddhist philosophy much annoyed the orthodox sections of the Sri Lankan Buddhist clergy.

During his student days in London he attended the Ommen Star Camps in Holland, and listened to the inspired insights of K, who was then in the splendour of his youth and early manhood. He told me that for many who attended those meetings, it was a deeply moving spiritual experience just to sit and gaze at the physical beauty of K, regardless of whether one managed to understand anything of what he was saying.

After ten years' service as Principal of Ananda Sastralaya in Kotte, Adikaram resigned his post, gave away his few possessions and lived like a sannyasin for the rest of his life. He had neither money in the form of savings nor was he entitled to receive a state pension. He was fond of quoting K's statement that there is no such thing as security. Intelligence, if one has it, is the only security. In the evening of his life he held the elevated and largely ceremonial position of Chancellor of the Sri Jayawardhanapura University. It was in this institution in 1980 that K addressed the university students.

Toward the latter part of his life Adikaram conceded that education was not the panacea for all social evils as he had once thought. Education makes us well-informed but not wise. When a criminal is educated, does he automatically become a better human being? It is not that criminals should not be educated, but what frequently happens is that education enables a criminal to continue performing his criminal deeds in a cleverer and more sophisticated form. Human nature cannot he changed via education; it can be done only when the psyche is purged of its selfish and anti-social traits, such as violence, ambition, hatred and envy. Only an inner psychological revolution can transform man's innate animalistic nature. This insight was something he had learnt from his great mentor — K.

The teachings of K profoundly shaped the mind of Adikaram and most of his close companions. I was already quite familiar with these teachings before I first met Adikaram. I was a student of Ananda College, Colombo, at the time and I vividly recall writing him a long letter and asking him whether he had heard of Krishnamurti. What prompted me to write such a letter? I had been reading a series of philosophical articles by Adikaram that were appearing in a Sinhalese daily called *Lankadeepa*. It struck me forcibly that although his writings expressed insights similar to those of K, he hardly mentioned K's name in them. A few days later I was pleasantly surprised to get a reply from him in which he acknowledged his debt to K. That was the beginning of our friendship — a close lifelong friendship of 30 odd years that only ended with his death. Sometimes we spent the whole day discussing subtle philosophical questions. Often we disagreed but he never failed me as a friend. He was always loyal and affectionate.

Adikaram and I travelled extensively in India, not merely with the purpose of listening to the discourses of K in Bombay and Poona, but also because we enjoyed visiting ashrams and ancient temples as well as places of great cultural interest such as Ajanta and Ellora. He was fond of going on Buddhist pilgrimages and at the site where the Buddha passed away he was moved to tears for he was overwhelmed by a strange presence. I should also mention something he told me concerning a visit to Ramana Maharishi at Tiruvannamalai. He had visited the sage alone and sat by him. No sooner had he been in the presence of Shri Ramana than he was immersed in a state of rapture or ecstasy.

Adikaram regarded the advent of K in the world as no ordinary event. For K was an Enlightened Sage, the sort of Teacher who rarely appears on earth. K was likened to a flower that blooms only once in a few thousand years. Therefore we never missed an opportunity to listen to K in various parts of India; it was as though we were travelling all the way to Benares some 2,500 years ago to listen to a discourse of the Buddha.

When Adikaram had his first audience with K in the privacy of a room, tears rolled down the cheeks of the learned doctor. He wept for a long time and K simply sat there, watching him in silence, without uttering a word. Adikaram suddenly stopped weeping on realising that he had been behaving like a child. He felt very shy that he had wept in K's presence. K then held Adikaram's hand consolingly and said: "Many visitors have cried after spending some time with me. It's a kind of sensitivity. When you see something extraordinarily beautiful or hear melodious singing, don't you feel like crying?"

Adikaram regarded K with the utmost reverence and always addressed him deferentially. Sometimes his lips quivered with emotion and his voice trembled when he had to converse with K. Once K took him to task and asked: "Why are you like this?" Adikaram answered : "Excuse me for saying it, but for me you are the Buddha."

K said: "Sir, I may be the Buddha but why are you afraid of me?"

The people of Sri Lanka should be particularly grateful to Adikaram because he was chiefly responsible for inviting K to Colombo and organising his many public talks and discussions during 1949, 1957 and 1980 when K visited the country for the last time. Consequently, thousands of men, women and children in Sri Lanka became acquainted with the teachings of this revolutionary religious teacher.

Given his Buddhist upbringing and his lifelong interest in Pali literature, Adikaram was naturally interested in the question of reincarnation. One of the highly treasured books in his personal library was *The Lives of Alcyone,* by Annie Besant and C.W. Leadbeater. This work is an investigation into K's past lives. One day he summoned enough courage to ask K whether these accounts of his previous lives were accurate. K remarked: "That won't help you." K's curt reply disconcerted Adikaram, who had been expecting an answer which clearly stated that the information in the book was either true or false. Often K was averse to dwell on questions relating to his early years, let alone his past lives, for he regarded them as matters of no consequence. Such questions bored him. The past is dead; it cannot be changed or revived; in any case, he had great difficulty in recalling anything beyond the immediate past. He was never good at remembering.

Adikaram devoted his energies to the dissemination of K's teachings throughout the length and breadth of Sri Lanka via his numerous writings, broadcasts and lectures. He was instrumental in the establishment of the Krishnamurti Centre of Sri

Lanka, which acquired legal status with the passage of Krishnamurti Centre, Sri Lanka (Incorporation) Act, No.70 of 1981 by the Parliament of the Democratic Socialist Republic of Sri Lanka. In a letter addressed to me and dated October 23rd 1981, he stated that "Ceylon will be the future repository of Krishnaji's teachings and all of us must work hard towards that end." He sincerely believed that it was Sri Lanka's special destiny to protect and safeguard K's teachings in the future, in the same way that this island had so lovingly cherished the teachings of the Buddha, after all the setbacks that Buddhism suffered in the land of its birth.

Adikaram declared that after studying K, he found that he was able to understand the teachings of the Buddha with greater clarity. I must admit that that was my own personal experience. The reason for the popularity of K's teachings in Sri Lanka is not solely attributable to Adikaram's efforts to disseminate them; I think the teachings would in any case have appealed to the Buddhist-inclined Sri Lankan public because doctrinally there is so much in common between the teachings of the Buddha and those of K. Both sages emphasised the importance of awareness — watching the thought process without distortion — as the only means to Liberation; both of them taught that there is no Saviour (none can save you save yourself); they both questioned the existence of anything that is permanent in the form of a soul or atman; above all, both Teachers showed that compassion alone will solve all human problems.

Adikaram was given to probing into himself with such intensity that long periods of rest became necessary to recover from all the attendant nervous strain. On January 19th 1981 he wrote me as follows: "Krishnaji's talks demand so much of energy that I always fall ill or feel very exhausted after each course of talks. So, I can well understand your exhaustion. I hope you are back to normal now."

Adikaram eagerly wished to predecease K, for he strongly felt that he could not possibly bear the pain of having to live in a gloomy world that was no longer blessed with the living presence of K. He had even identified himself with the two great disciples of the Buddha: namely, Sariputta and Mogallana, both of whom, alas, had predeceased the Buddha. On December 28th 1985 Adikaram died peacefully in his sleep. A few weeks later, on February 17th 1986, K also passed away. By an inexplicable turn of events, his wish to predecease K had strangely been fulfilled.

The cremation of Adikaram took place before a very large and representative gathering at which the Prime Minister of Sri Lanka delivered the funeral oration. One of the speakers was Dr. Anandatissa de Alwis, Minister of State, who said that Adikaram had a clear understanding of the philosophy of K. He was hailed as the greatest thinker of Sri Lanka in the twentieth century. He was planning to attend the last talks of K in Madras when he suddenly expired.

A dynamic interest in the teachings of K was the rich legacy that Adikaram left behind. Therefore I will have to refer to him several times more in the course of recording these reminiscences of K.

Personification of *metta*

Adikaram impressed on me again and again in 1953 that nothing in life is more important than studying

K's books, and also that nothing is sweeter than discussing K's teachings with like-minded friends, who are also enthusiastically interested in them. He insisted, nevertheless, that unless one closely associates with K, it is not possible to get a total picture of the man. He emphasised the danger of having a mere intellectual and academic understanding of the teachings. It is not enough be appreciative of K's boundless mind, because it is equally necessary to know K personally, and then see with one's own eyes that K is "the gentlest of creatures with a heart that is overflowing with compassion." K, he said, is the personification of metta. "Metta" in Buddhist terminology means loving kindness. Adikaram observed that those who only read his books or attend his public talks, such people invariably miss noticing the tender-hearted side of K's personality. "So get ready soon to travel to India. I'll introduce you to K whom I know well. I'll arrange an interview for you." Thereupon I stated that although his proposal was most appealing, I would sadly have to turn it down because, being a schoolboy, I lacked the money for a long journey.

"Oh, that's hardly a problem," he said, "because I'll pay all your expenses." I was very touched by his thoughtful and generous offer.

Mr. C. Jinarajadasa

In the course of our travels in India we met several persons who, at various times, had been closely associated with K, notably Mr. C. Jinarajadasa, who was then holding the position of President of the Theosophical Society. Affectionately called "Brother Raja", Jinarajadasa had played an important role in the early education of K. For he had been his private tutor. We accompanied Jinarajadasa on one of his evening walks through the beautiful gardens of the Theosophical Society in Madras. He walked extremely slowly for he was frail in body and seemed to be suffering from arthritis. He endeared himself to us because he spoke about K in a fond manner and made inquiries concerning K's health and whereabouts.

At that time, thanks to Jinarajadasa's interest in preserving things of great historic and sentimental value, the Theosophical Society housed a fascinating collection of articles that had once belonged to the boy K — his handwritten exercise books, textbooks, a few items of clothing and shoes. Even the dark locks of the boy were there. Many years later I wanted to make a photographic record of this collection. I was informed by the administrative officers of the society that they were unaware that such a collection had ever existed. Has it mysteriously disappeared?

I Meet Krishnamurti for the First Time

On the day of our interview with K, Adikaram closed his eyes and solemnly meditated for one hour. He informed me that before meeting K, it was so necessary to tidy up his mind and cleanse his stream of consciousness of self-centred thoughts. He advised me that I should also tidy up my own mind before meeting K. I laughingly remarked: "If K notices my untidy mind it doesn't matter!"

It was a bright and sunny afternoon when we arrived at the spacious bungalow of Mr. Patwardhan in Poona. Mr. D. Rajagopal greeted us on arrival. He requested us to send him newspaper clippings and articles from magazines as well as books relating to K. These he needed for preservation at his archives in Ojai, California. I should mention that these archives are now in the custody of the Krishnamurti Foundation of America.

We were ushered into K's room and requested to wait until his arrival. In the corner of this high-ceilinged small room was his old-fashioned bed, which was protectively covered with a white mosquito net. The soft carpet was strewn with jasmine flowers. Their sweet fragrance permeated the air. Suddenly he appeared. Immaculately dressed in a cream-coloured kurta and white pyjamas, K walked into the room and smilingly embraced Adikaram. It was nice seeing the hearty reunion of two old companions.

Adikaram introduced me to K: "Here is my friend Susunaga Weeraperuma from Colombo." I bowed respectfully and K warmly held my hands. Then, without uttering a word, all three of us sat on the carpet in a cross-legged position.

K sat right in front of me. He moved a little forward with the result that his knees were nearly touching mine. His face was very near mine and he started gazing intensely at my eyes. It was a fixed and prolonged focussing of attention on my eyes. It was like being exposed to a powerful beam from a searchlight. At first I experienced a sensation of uneasiness. Then I felt weak and dizzy and faintly. I turned away from him, and looked sideways in the direction of the veranda and garden. No sooner had I started looking out of the door than I was forced to look at his face again, directly, because his eyes were magnetic. I realised that I had failed to distract myself by looking elsewhere. So this time I looked him full in the face. I then realised that his piercing eyes were still observing me, watching every movement and gesture, as though my whole mind was being subjected to a searching X-ray. I started perspiring. I was vaguely conscious that something that had long been deeply embedded within my psyche was now melting away. The mind seemed somewhat unburdened and swifter in its capacity to perceive. We sat silently for about twenty minutes which appeared like twenty trying hours. And during this period, without saying anything, K continued looking at my eyes.

I had dabbled in hypnotism and it was obvious that K was not hypnotising me. I wondered whether K was trying to size-up my character. Years later, did he not say that he would never probe into the mind of another, for that would be like reading another's letter? Was K attempting to convey a message by non-verbal means? Adikaram commented that he, too, was puzzled, because during his long and intimate association with K, he had never previously seen him focussing his concentration upon a person for such a lengthy duration.

To this day I do not quite understand the significance, if any, of what actually transpired during that speechless spell with K. I discussed the matter with an eminent Theosophist. He opined that "it was an initiation". I blurted out: "Nonsense! Initiations are quite out of character. Did he not stress absolute self-reliance and rule out the possibility of any kind of external help in spiritual matters?"

Our meeting was supposed to be an interview but we were behaving like monks who had taken vows of silence. It occurred to me that I should soon start talking with K.

SW: Please may I ask you a question?

K : Go ahead.

SW: I wrote you a letter about a certain problem. Did you receive it?

K : I don't remember. What's your problem?

SW: I don't know whether it is right to call it a problem. Actually it is a situation of indecision. After reading your books I have been put into a dilemma.

K : Have you discussed it with Dr. Adikaram?

SW: I have done so. But I'm still confused. Recently I finished my college education. I've been a fairly good student. I got good marks and passed the examination. What I have to decide now is whether to enter an university or give up studying altogether. I am sure that my chances of finding employment will be remote unless I have an university degree. But if I continue studying with the intention of obtaining a degree, don't I run the risk of making my mind less sensitive? I'm eager to have a mind that is highly sensitive but amassing knowledge will increase my insensitivity and make the mind less pliable. I benefitted enormously by reading your books where you explain that knowledge is an hindrance. I've realised myself that knowledge makes the mind dull.

K : On the contrary! Knowledge makes the mind sharp and alert.

SW: I find that as I go on acquiring knowledge my character keeps on changing. My tastes change and so does my outlook. That innocent freshness of childhood is dropping away because I keep on changing. Isn't that a great pity?

K : What is changeable is not worth keeping.

SW: I'm not at all clear. What is your advice?

K : Look here. Sir, have you pots and pots of gold?

SW: No, I haven't.

K : Do you like carrying a begging bowl?

SW: Not at all.

K : Then you have to complete your education and find yourself a job. Go and get all the qualifications required for a job. Let us suppose that you are a student of engineering. Don't be ambitious and say "I am going to be the greatest engineer.". Be a good, efficient engineer: that is all. The desire to shine in society must be avoided. It is vulgar. Knowledge in itself is harmless but making use of knowledge as a means of self-fulfilment is what makes the mind dull.

SW: So you are not against knowledge?

K : Why, sir, don't we need more knowledge and better knowledge? A true scientist is always trying to extend the frontiers of knowledge. But when a scientist works hard with the intention of winning the Nobel prize, isn't he seeking his own glory?

SW: I still do not understand this question of when knowledge is dangerous and when it is useful.

K : Using knowledge for psychological purposes is harmful.

SW: In your talks you distinguish 'factual memory' from 'psychological memory'. What is factual is easy to understand. Please explain the term 'psychological memory'.

K : It is a fact that Dr. Adikaram is a Doctor of

Philosophy. That is factual memory. But the moment you regard him as a socially useful person because he happens to have an academic title, you have created psychological memory, haven't you? Now, can you view your friend directly, without looking at him through the screen of his title and reputation?

SW: I am still worried that my sensitivity may decrease as I grow older.

K : Be careful and ensure that it does not take place. I have to meet people but I am careful not to become insensitive.

Stimulated by K's words of wisdom, Adikaram ceased remaining quiet, and he decided to participate in the discussion.

A : My difficulty is that in the course of earning my livelihood by writing scientific articles, I tend to become insensitive. I wish I didn't have to work so that the mind is free to be in a state of heightened awareness all the time. If I didn't have to waste my energy away in materialistic pursuits I will have more energy for awareness.

K : Why are you separating the so-called material world from the so-called spiritual one? Have you tried translating your spiritual interest into a materialistic form so that there is no clash between the two spheres? The work of a genuine scientist does not stop with the examination of the external world. He should also examine his inner world. What you discover about yourself can be expressed in your scientific articles. If you are very observant of all the movements of your mind in your daily life, you will find that there will be a difference in the quality of your writing. You may become a more efficient writer. Your style may improve.

That year we thoroughly enjoyed the sparkling series of talks by K in Poona and Bombay. There is an unforgettable incident that occurred soon after a meeting in Poona one evening. A crowd of admirers and devotees encircled K and then a young lady placed a beautiful garland of flowers around his neck. In a fit of adoration she prostrated at the feet of K and kissed them. It was a traditional gesture of reverence, humility and submission. "Nothing of the sort!" exclaimed K pitifully, his voice rising in a crescendo. He clutched her arm and gently lifted her off the ground. Soon afterwards, he swiftly moved to a quiet corner of the garden and stood there all alone under a tree. The crowd quickly followed him there and encircled him again. His tearful and compassionate eyes gazed at their wretched faces. His face was transfigured by an expression of extreme tenderness. He seemed to be painfully conscious of the tremendous chasm between himself and these common people, who were not only burdened with sorrow but also poverty-stricken. Their agony contrasted sharply with the lucky lot of K, who had the comforts of this world and spiritual riches also.

A certain Vaisnavite sannyasin, aghast when K publicly told him that it was a stupid act to smear his body with holy ashes, was never seen again at the public talks. I felt very sorry for this ascetic, who was obviously upset by K's caustic remark. It frequently happened that K's forthright denunciations of tradition and religious beliefs put many people off the talks. Some refrained from asking him questions at meetings because they dreaded the possibility of their being publicly humiliated. All these categories of persons were the losers: first, they failed to realise that K was incapable of malice; second, they did not understand that K's words should be likened to a surgeon's lancet that hurts but also heals the patient.

In Bombay our leave-taking was brief because so many persons were impatiently waiting for their turn to talk with K. Adikaram invited him to Colombo for delivering another series of public lectures. K embraced us and said: "Go home and take a good rest. You have listened to the talks. Sirs, shout it from the housetops."

The Sage who Speaks from Direct Experience

The Krishnamurti Reception Committee was responsible for inviting K to Sri Lanka in 1957. I was a very active member of this body. The main functions of this committee were to organize his meetings in Colombo and to look after K during the time he was going to be our honoured guest. At the inaugural meeting of the committee, a moving speech was made by Dr. Adikaram, who was the chairman of the committee. "During the next few weeks," he said, "we will be the custodians of Krishnaji who is the greatest treasure in the world." Some of the committee members were assigned specific duties. For instance, I was requested to find as quickly as possible a suitable house in the city of Colombo for K; to attend to K's personal needs and also to give the widest possible publicity to K's visit by writing articles about him for the local press.

On the 31st of December 1956 both *The Ceylon Observer* and *The Ceylon Daily News* carried my article on K. What follows is a slightly altered version of that article:

KRISHNAMURTI: A SAGE WHO SPEAKS FROM DIRECT EXPERIENCE

Jiddu Krishnamurti is a unique personality. He is not a philosopher in that he has not formulated a school of thought or beliefs; he is not a poet though he has written some exquisite poetry; he is not a great writer of books, nor is he the founder of a new religion though religions have sprung from men like him. The truth is that Krishnamurti is so universal that he is beyond classification.

With no organization to back him and with no "followers", for more than 20 years he has travelled widely in Europe, India, Australia and America, lecturing and meeting thousands from all walks of life. Few have not drawn water from his well. What is overwhelming in Krishnamurti and what is his strange mission?

It is a tribute to the greatness of Dr. Annie Besant that she foresaw the spiritual genius of an obscure Indian boy of 12. She proclaimed Krishnamurti to the world as the Messiah. His admirers founded an international Order of the Star in the East to salute the arrival of the World Teacher. Yet the striking individuality of Krishnamurti was seen in his renunciation of the role prepared for him and the fact that he successfully withstood the influences of powerful personalities like Mr. Leadbeater and Mrs. Besant of the Theosophical Society. Truth cannot be organized; and Krishnamurti pointed out the pointlessness of spiritual organizations because people become more interested in organizations than in what these are supposed to propagate.

Not from Books

The source of Krishnamurti's deep understanding is not scholarship that is dependent on books. On one occasion Krishnamurti referred to the unhappy days when he was a schoolboy, and especially to the difficulties experienced because of his inability to recall what had been learned. He said that the things the teachers told him at school just went in at one ear and came out at the other. He was never good at passing examinations. When he went into the examination hall he used to get frightened and forget everything he had studied. So up to a very late age in his life he just did the things they asked him to do. He did everything like one in a dream. He is careful not to "contaminate" his mind with the ideas of other philosophers.

If Krishnamurti's teachings happen to have been uttered by other sages, mystics and teachers, it is accidental because he speaks from direct and first-hand knowledge. Besides, reality which is ever-new can never be faced through the experiences or ideas of others. Organized religion, he declared, is "the frozen thought of man", the material out of which he constructs temples and churches; it has become a solace for those in a state of fear and an opiate for those in a state of sorrow. But God or truth, he insists, is far beyond the demands of thought and emotion.

It is significant that most of his talks begin with a few introductory remarks on the art of listening. At once he seems to go directly to the very source of all problems. One does not understand unless one listens. To listen without acceptance or rejection, to listen without belief or disbelief is arduously difficult, because one responds to a situation according to one's past conditioning and background of beliefs, philosophies, social conventions, prejudices and the like. Does one ever listen without interpretation? So long as one reacts to the pattern of past conditioning is there ever a moment of pure experience?

World of No "I"

The unconscious is the reservoir of one's urges, hopes, fears, anxieties, racial prejudices and the like. Thinking, voluntarily or involuntarily is directed and propelled by this vast background. The ways of the mind are such that everything is interpreted by this background. If anything really new is experienced, a name is given to it, and this otherwise fresh experience is once again incorporated with accumulated thought, the known. Therefore, reality, the unknown, is never knowable through the mind, which is composed of thought, the known. "Thought can only think about what is; it can never know." Reality, then, is in the interval between two thoughts.

If this fact can be seen — the inability to experience anything new by the mind, shocking though it is, a fundamental transformation will instantly occur — the complete rejection of memory, the bundle of the entire thought process. The question may be asked: can the "thinker" dissociate itself from thought? The question does not arise because the thought process actually creates the illusion of a "thinker" or an "I". Since the thought process creates the "I", the dissolution of that process will eventually bring about the disappearance of the illusory "I". Krishnamurti belongs to a world that has torn aside the prison walls of "I" and is therefore in a state of creativity every moment. One can only speculate about this state; Krishnamurti has variously described it — Reality, Love, God, Truth, etc.

Truth cannot be sought after since the known cannot comprehend the unknown. But the rejection of the known makes one receptive to the unknown, that comes unsought. Creative thinking will eventually suggest the path of creative action: the creative and intelligent mind will spontaneously identify itself with the right course, for only an uncreative and unintelligent mind will have choice, and therefore "free-will".

Childlike Simplicity

So long as man is obsessed by the illusion of "self", he seeks self-fulfilment, psychological security and becomes greedy and possessive. Genuine selfless love is only possible with the absence of thought that creates the self. Krishnamurti once watched a passing train with the genuine delight of a new experience. The sight of a withered branch moved him to tears. This childlike simplicity suggests an extraordinary sensitivity and openness to everything, be it the beauty of a sunset or the misery of a beggar, every moment of his existence. Such a man with a poet's capacity for every shade of experience cannot feel the boredom and monotony of modern life. Such a man will have an infinite capacity to feel and love and an intelligence sharper than a razor's edge.

Krishnamurti will remain an enigma so long as his teachings are measured by the yardstick of man's conditioning. The conditioned mind, the moment it faces the fact of being conditioned, is thereupon instantaneously free. Similarly, if the fact of interpretation according to one's likes and dislikes of Krishnamurti's teachings is faced fully, in that very process, the wonderful message of Krishnamurti may be grasped.

Dr. Adikaram highly commended my article. "I like it very much," he said, "but it has created a problem. After the article was published, the applications for tickets for the Colombo Town Hall lectures have increased by the hundreds. We have run out of tickets and there isn't enough room in the hall to accommodate all those who want to listen to Krishnaji." Then with characteristic efficiency he solved this problem. As a prominent public personality Dr. Adikaram exercised his influence over the Sri Lankan government, and with the assistance of Mr. I.M.R.A. Iriyagolle, who was a parliamentarian and an ardent admirer of K, Radio Ceylon was persuaded to broadcast all the talks of K for the benefit of listeners throughout Sri Lanka and India.

In crowded cities such as Colombo, where there is an acute shortage of housing, it is well nigh impossible to find a landlord who is willing to lease a spacious bungalow with a nice garden for just one month. The required bungalow, we insisted, should also be situated in a quiet neighbourhood with lots of trees. It was thought that only a bungalow with these conditions would be a suitable enough resting place for K. No sooner had I started searching for such a residence than I met a landlord who offered me one with all the aforementioned requirements. I was much surprised. It was a newly built elegant bungalow, bordering a shady sylvan cemetery in the vicinity of treelined Jawatta Road. The landlord said: "It will be an honour if he lives in my house even for a day and sanctifies it." K lived there for several weeks. In life whenever I eagerly wanted something for myself I have had to struggle hard to get it. But whenever I tried to supply K's very few physical needs, what was sought was always very easily and mysteriously provided!

At the Colombo airport a huge crowd had been standing in the scorching sun for several hours with the intention of greeting K. When the aeroplane landed the people stampeded to the tarmac to see him. K was given a warm welcome. When K walked near us a loud voice exclaimed: "What a Divine face!" K chanced to hear that remark and he immediately covered his face with his wide canvas umbrella with the result that many onlookers failed even to catch a glimpse of him that afternoon.

A press photographer requested K to pose for a photograph. "I am so sorry," said K apologetically and added, "I have declined to be photographed in New York and London also."

The photographer implored K to grant his request: "Please may I take just one picture?"

"Why don't you take a picture of a tree or a mountain instead?" said K as he quickly walked away.

K had to fill out an official form at the airport. After carefully answering all the questions, he was confronted with a minor problem. For a long time he was gazing vacantly at the dotted line where he was required to sign. He did not seem to know what to do. K actually forgot his own name! Then a member of his entourage spoke to K in a whisper: "You must write J. Krishnamurti there."

"Ah, thank you," said K gratefully, who signed the document forthwith.

His name was indeed a very prestigious one in the world but to him it was nothing more than a mere word given him by society. In this respect, he was conspicuously different from the rest of us because we are inseparably chained to our names. Who likes to discard his name, especially if it is associated with various successes and glories? My name is virtually synonymous in my mind with my ego and hence I will always remember it.

Press Conference in Colombo

A few hours after K's arrival in Colombo, when the trying tropical heat had been followed by the cool evening breezes, there was an open air press conference on the roof garden of K's abode. A galaxy of foreign and local journalists had assembled there. They were seated on chairs and benches and some of them were dangerously perched on a parapet wall. All were anxiously awaiting the arrival of K who was expected to sit on a majestic thronelike chair. The moment K appeared on the scene, looking frail and tired, those present rose deferentially.

"Please don't bother to stand up. Please remain seated," K urged the journalists. He always seemed pained whenever he was held in respect. He discouraged the showing of any kind of deference to him. Next K was directed to the imposing chair that had been specially prepared for him.

"No, thank you," he said austerely. After refusing to use that chair, he looked around and selected an ordinary wooden stool instead. That simple act of humility told us a great deal about the character of the man and the quality of his teaching.

A dashing young journalist asked the following personal question: "Do you regard yourself as a fully enlightened being?" K smiled and answered: "It is not at all important whether I happen to be enlightened or not enlightened. What is of importance is whether you have cared to examine all that I am talking about and found my statements to be true in the light of your own understanding. You ask this question, don't you, because deep down within yourself you are seeking certainty. This desire for certainty shows that you are actually interested in security. The mind is everlastingly seeking security through theories and explanations. Now if I say 'I am enlightened' then you will take me seriously and readily accept all my statements. Surely you must find out yourself whether what I am saying is sane or otherwise. No one can help you to do that. You alone have to do it. The speaker has no authority. If you have understood something very deeply, profoundly, then the truth of what you have understood will operate in your life. Truth is its own authority."

The sprightly journalists bombarded K with many questions. The following is an edited report of some of the questions and answers.

You say that a person should be self-reliant in spiritual matters. If you really mean what you say, why do you waste your time giving talks?

K: Sir, why does a flower give scent? A flower cannot help perfuming the air. When you see something very clearly, don't you want to share that clarity with others? I talk because I cannot help doing so. I do not talk with the intention of helping others. That would be too patronizing. I talk simply because there is a song in my heart. And I will sing regardless of whether anybody cares to listen to what I am saying. A flower blossoms because that is its glory, its fulfilment, its dharma. The flower is not concerned whether passers-by enjoy it or ignore it.

Is your teaching for the select few or the many? Do you believe that your elitist philosophy is going to become popular with the masses of people?

K: Why have you separated yourself from the masses? You are the world and the world is you. You may be lucky enough to be living in a palace with lots of servants but are you psychologically different from the so-called masses? Whether you are rich or poor, whether you live in the East or West, whether you live in Ceylon or Siberia, are your minds basically different? Wherever one lives, whatever one's situation in life, we all suffer and die, don't we? It is important to realize that our minds are all the same. The mind is its consciousness and nothing else. And what is your mind other than a collection of your fears, hopes, ambitions, hurts and beliefs?

You have asked if the teaching is likely to appeal to the ordinary people. Are you saying that a peasant cannot understand me? Is a peasant psychologically different from yourself? Intelligence is not a gift because within each individual is the capacity to understand.

You have talked and talked for so many years but

the world remains unchanged. Please comment on this statement.

K: People go to the river and take what they want. Some go with a pitcher. Some only drink in sips. So the question is really not what is offered but what is taken. The river has plenty of water but you take only a handful of it, depending on the temporary satisfaction of your immediate needs. You are easily satisfied. You are not deeply discontented. You are not thirsty enough to drink the pure waters in large amounts.

Why don't you have a recognized body of followers in accordance with the practice of other gurus?

K: Don't you know that it is the followers who destroy their guru? The followers exploit their guru and the guru in turn exploits his followers and so their relationship becomes one of mutual exploitation! Thank God, I have no followers! First of all find out why you want to follow another. Therein you will discover something about yourself. Why follow anyone, including the speaker? You desire to follow because you are in the dark. And when you become a follower, aren't you still in the dark? Therefore must you not be a light unto yourself?

We are such weaklings that we need leaders.

K: Isn't this practice of following another that has made you weak?

It has been reported in the press that you do not read. Is this true?

K: I sometimes read *Time* magazine to keep abreast of world events. I also read detective stories and crime. That is all.

Aren't you concerned that your pure mind will be conditioned by the corrupting influences of escapist literature such as detective novels?

K: Corrupt the mind? (laughter). Good Lord! Nothing corrupts! The mind remains unsullied, innocent, fresh and young.

What about sacred literature? Do you study them?

K: I find that religious and philosophical books bore me. I don't read such stuff.

Imageless seeing

For the entire duration of K's stay in Colombo, I spent most of my time in the peaceful atmosphere of the bungalow where he lived. My tiny room downstairs was directly below K's spacious and airy room upstairs. Every morning I used to clean the house and decorate the drawing room with nice sweet-smelling flowers. K was very fond of flowers, especially flowers that belonged to the jasmine family. Fortunately there was an abundance of flowers because visitors were always bringing carnations and roses for K as an expression of their respect and affection for him. So we had a huge vase containing lots of flowers on the ground floor near the stairs. Whenever K passed that vase he stopped briefly to admire the beauty of the flowers and to experience their fragrance with joy.

One morning after breakfast, when K was explaining to us the nature of pure perception, he asked: "Have you ever looked at a flower, not partially, but *completely?*" When we all replied in the negative, K proceeded to elucidate his question thus: "After glimpsing a flower, the mind likes to interfere with that experience by giving it a name. If you are a botanist, the flower is immediately classified and given a Latin name. You say it belongs to this genus or that species. You also verbalize your experience by saying 'the flower is red', 'the flower is lovely' and so forth. Now, after glimpsing a flower, continue looking at it non-botanically, without seeing it through the screen of words or images. Have you tried looking at a flower in a state of total emptiness? Have you ever tried dropping all images so that your perception is direct and undistorted?"

K's words came as a shock because he showed us the utterly conditioned state of our minds. It is not that we are incapable of pure perception. Apparently, we all have flashes of pure perception, momentary glimpses of extraordinary clarity, but the difficulty is that these soon get overpowered by the interpretative mechanism of the mind.

Undisturbed Seclusion

Although K and I lived in the same house, it was only seldom that I was in close proximity to him. This was because K had all his meals — breakfast, lunch and dinner — in the undisturbed seclusion of his room, except on the few occasions when he was invited out for dinner. Every morning at eleven o' clock he was given a glassful of buttermilk; then in the afternoons at three o'clock he was provided with fruit juice. Whenever I took these drinks into his room, I noticed that he was either laboriously writing with a pencil or resting in bed. He spent much time relaxing. He liked to lie down in a horizontal position and remain motionless in the savasana or corpse posture for a very long time. His face looked particularly serene when he performed this asana.

Some persons were rather disappointed that they were denied the opportunity of meeting K. The then secretary of K, Mr. R. Madhavachari, minimized the number of persons who were allowed to meet K. He reasoned that K should be given every opportunity to recuperate after his illness in Madras. But long before we were informed about K's state of health, some of us, including myself, had deliberately turned down invitations to meet K because of our realization that he needed a long period of convalescence.

Often K used to draw the curtains of his windows and thereby shut out all daylight. Nearly everyday he spent several hours in pitch-darkness. This practice may have arisen from the need to protect his hypersensitive eyes from the direct rays of the sun. There may have been other reasons for it. I have read that total darkness is conducive to probing the profoundest depths of one's being.

Real Renunciation

It was a lovely evening and K got inside a car because he was going to be taken for a drive along the seafront. Just when the vehicle started moving, he was hailed in the street by a bald, clean-shaved German swami, who was dressed in a dhoti. Their conversation lasted for a very short time but it is worth reporting:

Swami: Excuse me for disturbing you. May I speak with you for a moment?

K : You may do so.

Swami: I have been a sannyasi for many years. I now live in an ashram in the Jaffna area. Before coming to this island, I was practising meditation in a Tibetan monastery. Sir, I have sincerely searched and searched for Liberation. Still I haven't found it. I gave up my country. I gave up my family and friends. I gave away all my possessions. I own nothing. I even renounced my name. There is nothing more left in me to renounce.

K : But have you given up trying to become virtuous?

The swami was completely stunned by the unpleasant truth about himself which K pointed out.

That night before going to bed, I deeply considered K's words and thereafter jotted down a few observations in my notebook: It is the ego that hopes to buy spiritual glory with the coin of virtue. It is the ego that desires to 'renounce' in its endless quest for greatness. When monks 'renounce', do they not expect spiritual rewards in return? But the person who is not attached to anything, the genuine renunciant, acting motivelessly, joyously gives up the world without a struggle.

Intelligence is the Only Security

One afternoon we noticed the presence of an unexpected visitor at the entrance to the house. He was a beggar in rags, who was carrying a drum and a stringed instrument. I gave him a few rupees and requested him to sing some Sinhalese folk songs. He started singing cheerfully and loudly with the result that K opened his bedroom window and leaned forward to hear the melodious chants. K listened with rapt attention for half an hour. It surprised us very much when K suddenly appeared and affectionately hugged the beggar. K thanked the poor man and presented him with a clean white towel and a pair of pyjama trousers that belonged to him. This was not the first occasion when I had seen such acts of spontaneous generosity on the part of K. Soon after the beggar's departure, my friend, Mr Abeysekara, conversed with K in the lounge downstairs:

A: If we have rightly understood your teachings, shouldn't we all end up as beggars ourselves?

K: Physical security must not be confused with psychological security. We all need decent clothes, the right food and a roof above our heads, don't we? That kind of security is essential to keep the body healthy. But do we need the satisfaction of having so many gods and idols and beliefs? So when you seek psychological security in this way, you are chasing illusions, aren't you?

A: You have said that intelligence is the only security.

K: That's right. So try throwing off all your attachments.

A: Being a beggar and walking the streets is not at all easy. No proud person would be prepared to beg. I would like to become a beggar because having to beg for my needs will teach me humility.

K: Humility cannot be acquired by behaving like a beggar. Humility cannot be cultivated by the cunning intellect. Just see that it is your pride which says 'I want to be humble'. The carefully cultivated humility of the religious people is really a disguised form of pride. So what is important is seeing yourself as you are, right now, seeing the fact of *what is*, without bothering about *what should be*.

Nationalism is Poison

At an informal discussion meeting, which was attended by a few ardent nationalists, K showed us very clearly how the spirit of nationalism in our minds was responsible for the disintegration of humanity:

"The problems of the world can be solved only if you approach them with an outlook that is wholesome. When you worship the flag, aren't you separating otherwise friendly people? The very primitive sentiment that 'my country is superior to yours' can be traced back to man's tribal past, when his behaviour was governed by tribal loyalties. Nationalism is one of the principal causes of war. Do you see for yourselves that nationalism is poison?"

Soon after this meeting, there was a programme of Sinhalese music, which had been organized by Mr. Abeysekara with the assistance of Radio Ceylon artistes. K was the chief guest at this free concert which was open to the public. The concert began with the strains of the well-known national anthem of Sri Lanka, the opening lines of which are 'Namo, Namo Matha'. K smiled and asked ironically: "Ladies and gentlemen, shouldn't we all stand up when the national anthem is played?"

Stately Behaviour

Mr. Dudley Senanayake, a distinguished politician and a former Prime Minister of Sri Lanka, visited K one morning. A stocky man wearing an elegant business suit, he arrived in a luxurious limousine and was all the time surrounded by members of his entourage. He was sporting his famous pipe and enjoying the fact that he was still in the limelight. What a contrast he was to the slim and shy K, who was dressed in the simplest of clothes!

DS: I'm pressed for time this morning. Therefore I will ask only one question. Do you think it advisable for me to reenter politics and aspire to the highest political office in the land?

K : Have you tried finding out why you are attracted by politics? Do you sincerely wish to raise the living conditions of the people or do you desire to raise yourself? What unknown forces are driving you? Is it personal ambition and the desire for prestige? Don't you feel terribly important when you hold a powerful position?

DS: That's enough! Goodbye.

The short interview ended abruptly because the statesman walked away in a bad temper.

Selflessness

Buddhist monks and Hindu swamis have frequently felt a strong affinity for the teachings of K but rarely did rabbis and Christian priests evince much regard for them. Therefore it gladdened one's heart to see a bearded Christian clergyman calling on K. After their private meeting, the priest reported as follows: "Krishnamurti is a very charming person. He made me look at the symbol of the cross in a completely different light. The crucifix that is worn round my neck is not an ornament but a sign of my Christian faith. As you no doubt know, our Lord Jesus was crucified. He was nailed and left to die as a form of punishment. We believe that the death of Christ was the supreme act that saved the world. We were set free from the jaws of death by the holy cross. But Krishnamurti taught me the occult significance of the cross. He said that the cross symbolized the destruction of the "I" or the self. When you cancel the letter "I" with a horizontal line you get the cross."

The Great Silence

A few of his friends always accompanied K whenever he went for walks in the busy streets of Colombo or right out in the countryside. Such an arrangement became necessary because his sense of direction was not good enough. He tended to forget his way back home, if he ventured out on his own without a guide. Often during his walks, he was inclined to stop here and there for long periods, for the purpose of leisurely observing the various things that interested him, with the result that he lost all sense of chronological time.

K usually walked briskly with long steps. With his head held high he would swing his long arms as he moved. He was always conspicuous because of his erect bearing and solemn mien. I was for ever puzzled by the way strangers reacted to K when he walked the streets. Even people who knew nothing about him felt the need to look at him. Men, women and children stopped what they were doing and their attention involuntarily turned to K. Their behaviour may have been caused by a certain unconscious attraction to the purity and extraordinariness of K.

K tirelessly pointed out the shortcomings of those who associated with him. For example, a certain young man had the habit of grabbing leaves and flowers and thereafter crushing them. One day when we were walking in a tropical forest and enjoying its colourful flowers and birds, this man started uprooting shrubs. K told him to be wide-awake all the time, especially when he felt the urge to destroy vegetation. K said: "Sir, are you aware that you are now giving vent to your anger and frustration?"

During our walks together one hardly got an opportunity for asking K a question because nearly all the time he was the eager questioner. He was very curious to learn from others. He knew a lot about gardening and automobiles but his mind was uninformed about many things. However, he was equally interested in every field of knowledge: he had no overriding special interests. The universality of his mind was such that he had the capacity to focus his undivided attention on any subject or problem.

The mysterious loveliness of the heavens fascinated K. He was conversant with astronomy and from his balcony upstairs he loved to stargaze at night. He questioned us about certain stars but unfortunately we did not know the answers. One of the things that K asked us to do is as follows: "Look at the morning star before the dawn. Meditate alone and become conscious of the great silence and beauty that pervades the entire universe."

The Infinite

K fully understood the futility of attempting to describe the indescribable. He was primarily concerned with the removal of obstacles, the unconditioning of the mind so to speak, so that the mind itself is metamorphosed into a purified receptacle for the visitation of the Infinite. In this respect, K was so very much like the Buddha, who also had refused to make positive statements about the Infinite but preferred alluding to its nature by a series of negative declarations. Nirvana was indirectly called the unborn, the uncreated, the unoriginated and the unformed. The conditioned mind, according to K, is incapable of communicating with the unconditioned state or the otherness. Between the conditioned and the unconditioned no relationship whatsoever is possible.

The evening when K referred to the Infinite with intense feeling is one of my happiest recollections. "Believe me, I only see a fragment of the Infinite," he said. Then after wiping the tears off his ecstatic face, he added: "You cannot see it all. Such is the immensity of the Infinite."

Wholehearted Devotion

Over the many years that I associated with K, it so happened that I met some of his ardent devotees. Most of them were of Indian origin, but the person whose wholehearted devotion to K was of unparalleled intensity was a remarkable English woman called Lady Emily Lutyens. The wife of Sir Edwin Lutyens who was one of the outstanding architects of this century, Lady Emily took a maternal interest in the welfare of K. Her autobiography, *Candles in the Sun* (London: Rupert Hart-Davis, 1957) is more than a mere narration of the course of her life, because it is also a moving account of the early years of K's life in which she was personally involved, right from the time he first came to England as a boy of fifteen. This book tells the story of why the author joined the

Theosophical Society in 1910 and why she left it twenty years later. Lady Emily wrote that "the one all absorbing thought for me in this life is the coming of the Great Teacher" and she regarded K as "the perfect flower of humanity".

It was during my student days in Leeds and London that Lady Emily became friendly with me. How I admired her burning passion for the personality and teachings of K! I received a letter from her with touching references to K:

2 Hyde Park Street,
London W2
Oct: 7: 60

Dear Mr. Weeraperuma,

I was so pleased to get your charming letter. I am glad my book about Krishnaji interested you. I think you would also be very interested in a book by my youngest daughter Mary Lutyens (Mrs. J.G. Links). It tells her interest in Krishnaji & his brother Nitya who died of T.B.

I was very devoted to Krishnaji from the first moment that he came to England & have always regarded him as my son & he calls me Mother. There are many sides to him or rather many personalities in one frame.

He was in London last spring on his way to Ojai & came to see me every day. He had been ill in India & on his way had been to a vegetarian hospital in Switzerland & told me he would return there in August. He was to give six or eight lectures in Ojai but had to cancel the last ones because of his health. Then he went with

Mr. Rajagopal to the hills. I heard he was much better but I have had no letter from him or direct news — so I don't know why he has changed all his plans.

Although, as you mention, I suffered for some years from acute depression, as every thing I believed & hoped seemed to have crumbled round me & I was in a dark tunnel. But now I have come out into the sun again. But I fear that the reason is not that I know more but rather that I now know nothing about any thing! The world is upside down all nations *dis*-united. So I feel rather like the spectator of a circus!

I am 86 & rather feeble so I hope that I shall soon leave this world — for what? I don't know.

On this cheerful note I had better say goodbye & thank you again for your nice letter. If I have any happy news about Krishnaji & his next movements I will let you know.

Yours sincerely
Emily Lutyens

Is the Krishnamurti Foundation necessary?

I have always maintained that the creation of the Krishnamurti Foundation Trust was a colossal mistake.

My disillusionment at the Krishnamurti Foundation's lack of respect for K's wishes will be discussed elsewhere in this book. Please refer to the section titled *Sayings of J. Krishnamurti* (pages 99-103).

My views about the Foundation were frankly expressed in a confidential communication from London, which was addressed to K in 1968:

My dear Krishnaji,

Some of your friends, including myself, are astounded and alarmed by your recent decision to establish a new organization called the Krishnamurti Foundation. I seriously doubt whether you really want such a body to come into existence. Probably certain persons put pressure on you to accept this institution. Am I right?

All your life you were cautioning us against spiritual organizations. You were asking us not to get lost and confused in them but to remain wholly alone and simple. Your dissolution of the Order of the Star was therefore well in accord with the spirit of your noble teachings.

You have of course restricted the activities of the Foundation which, I believe, is going to be only a kind of secretariat and an administrative body. You have made it abundantly clear that the Foundation is definitely not a spiritual organization. But what is the guarantee that the Foundation's administrators will not overstep their bounds someday and behave with priestly power and arrogance? That will happen in all probability. All the great religious teachers were betrayed by those who claimed to be the guardians of their doctrines.

Your teachings have the quality of immortality. Their intrinsic merit alone will ensure their survival. Your teachings will always be valued, not because of the existence of the Foundation but in spite of it. One of the things I learnt from you is that Truth does not need a protector because it is capable of protecting itself.

Was there ever a need to appoint trustees to look after the works of men of genius like Shakespeare, Goethe or Kalidasa? Without the assistance of a foundation, have not the Vedas and the Upanishads succeeded in illuminating mankind for centuries? How ridiculous if one were required to get permission from a foundation for the purpose of quoting from these masterpieces of Hindu literature! Fortunately such crippling restrictions did not exist and consequently Indian civilization flourished.

The moment you have trustees with proprietorial and financial interests in your teachings, then what happens? Will they not abuse their powers for their own selfish ends?

Is the Foundation going to be run by saints or ordinary mortals with all their human weaknesses?

If you are planning to recruit angels to run it, then let us have more Krishnamurti Foundations. But if celestial personnel cannot be found, will it not be better to dissolve the Krishnamurti Foundation?

Yours affectionately,
S. Weeraperuma

K did not reply my letter and I wondered what happened to it. Several months later we met accidentally while he was taking a walk along the Thames. After exchanging pleasantries, I asked him whether he had received my letter.

K said: "Yes, I did. It is quite a sensible letter."

The Personality of Krishnamurti

During the first few years of my association with K, I remember that he seemed like an enigma because of his many-sidedness. It was as though several different individuals were embodied in K. I wondered how such seeming contradictory qualities could possibly coexist in a single human being. Later, as my understanding of him deepened, I realized that the diverse elements in his character were all nicely blended with the result that his personality had a harmonious wholeness. Let us now consider certain salient features of his personality.

One of the most endearing traits in K's character was the concerned way in which he listened to people who sought his company because they wanted to discuss with him their personal problems. K listened with such whole-hearted attention and sympathy as though your personal problems were the only problems in the world and nothing else mattered. One felt that he was more interested in understanding and solving your problems than you were in doing so yourself. He loved to investigate a question thoroughly and uncover its many facets. His hands shook with emotion as he investigated and spoke with passionate eagerness. Who would not feel honoured to become the object of such interest? That was the respectful and loving manner in which he treated one and all, regardless of whether the person visiting him was the Prime Minister, a learned pundit or a destitute pariah.

It is worth looking at a typical example of K's kind-hearted advice which was given during interviews. My American friend, David Rodriguez, who listened to K for many years at Saanen and elsewhere, vividly described his interview with K: ' "...Learn to understand how you are influenced by money, sex, the drive for power, security, fame and all the stupidities of this petty little brain!" he said emphatically while tapping me on the head. "Go into it intensely, thoroughly, see through the whole thing. You can only do it for yourself. Neither I nor anybody else can do it for you. And when you do, the job is over!" He said all this with vivacity, sitting as close as possible right in front of me, looking me in the eyes, shaking my arm and pushing me occasionally as if trying to awaken me.'

At the end of a hectic discussion meeting that had lasted for well over two hours, K looked worn-out. He wanted to leave but certain members of the audience persisted in asking him further questions. He patiently answered them but none seemed to understand what he said. K then resorted to using simpler language but still everyone was in the dark. A gentleman sighed and addressed K: "Sir, what will you do when a man is incapable of understanding you?"

K replied: "I will hold his hand."

It was a touching reply. Even when every attempt to communicate with others had failed, K never stopped expressing his affection. K also never lost heart despite the existence of so many psychological barriers to understanding.

A small pale emaciated beggar girl from the slums of Adyar accosted K in the road one evening. She was barely twelve years old. She sobbed out the whole sad story that she had not eaten anything for the last two days. She extended her bony brown hands and begged for some money. K immediately thrust his hands into his pockets and found that they were empty. That was not surprising because K hardly handled money. All that he possessed at the time of this incident was a clean white cotton handkerchief. K then presented her with his handkerchief. He affectionately gave the girl a pat and walked away.

Some of my friends and I were relaxing after enjoying a meal with K. He excused himself and went into the kitchen. When he returned he was carrying a huge tray with several cups containing a tasty cereal drink. It was a beverage he had specially prepared for us. Like an old fashioned waiter in a high-class restaurant, K politely bowed down before each guest and then handed the drink. After serving the drink he bowed down again. K did not consider wait ing on us to be infra dig. For him no job was menial. We were all struck by K's total lack of a feeling of self-importance. He treasured no image of himself as a great man or a great sage. In fact, he had no image of himself at all.

This imageless state of being was especially evident during the memorable hour I spent with K at a quiet house in Wimbledon during the early 1960s. On this occasion I took along my Dutch friend, Dr. Robert Powell, a writer of books on scientific and spiritual subjects as well as the teachings of K. After our interview, Robert made a profound observation: "When talking to Krishnamurti I got the impression that within himself there was no psychological person. All I sensed was a state of nothingness. You could walk through him as it were."

K was undoubtedly an outstanding spiritual master but he viewed mundane matters with a certain innocent childlike simplicity. I found, for instance, that he either failed to understand complex financial problems or understood them superficially.

If a man were to cheat me out of my money or tell me lies, I would naturally form an unfavourable opinion of him. The mental picture or image I have of that person will influence my attitude towards him. Probably I would dislike him and also become very cautious in my future dealings with him. Thus the image will shield me from becoming again the victim of his dishonesty. Although images discolour the mind and cause bitter feelings, they are a protective warning in a world that is replete with crooked deceitful people. Now K formed neither favourable nor unfavourable images of the persons who associated with him. His obliviousness of their treachery and other shortcomings was such that he was sometimes deceived by some of them. A few exploited K's prestigious reputation for their financial and personal advantage. One day I was so upset by some of K's decisions that I went to him and blurted out my views: "Why do you pick the wrong kind of persons to run your schools and organizations? Why do you select people who are hell-bent on furthering their personal ambitions, although they may have some interest in your teachings?"

It was so typical of K that he calmly listened to my accusations without necessarily agreeing nor disagreeing with them.

Probably a few of those who listened to K seriously and experimented sincerely with his teachings were animated by what could best be described as that passion, fire or intensity, which was the hallmark of K. I noticed, however, that our fire was short-lived whereas K's was an eternal one. His fire sprang from an unseen and unknown source and it never left him. How we relied on K to rekindle that intensity within ourselves! I will never forget something he said when we accidentally met in a public park: "Sir, don't hesitate. Don't vacillate. Go at it with fury."

His Subtle Sense of Humour

"Krishnamurti is a stern and humourless speaker who is given to occasional outbursts of harsh words," complained a Christian missionary after listening to one of K's discourses at the Society of Friends in Euston. This clergyman from London had attended the lecture only because I had persuaded him to do so. He grumbled about his wasted evening at the meeting and added: "Why is Krishnamurti so angry? A saintly man should be soft-spoken, shouldn't he?"

"A man who speaks and acts with passion," I explained, "is not necessarily angry. Anger springs from hate and violence and malice but K's strong words originate in loving concern for suffering humanity. Was Jesus acting angrily when he went into the Temple and drove away those who were desecrating it by buying and selling there? On that occasion didn't Jesus resort to condemnatory language by accusing them of using the Temple as a 'hideout for thieves'?" I never met this man of the cloth again. At Christmas time I posted him a copy of K's *The First and Last Freedom.* In a letter of thanks he stated that he had revised his opinion of K after reading this book. He wrote: "Jesus, I am sure, was also a radical religious preacher, like Krishnamurti, but what we get now is a watered-down teaching from the church. Both Jesus and Krishnamurti seem to have the same facial features. That is interesting."

Whenever K mounted a platform to speak, there was a certain subtle change in his personality. His self-effacing shyness fell into abeyance; he had the manner of an aloof speaker who did not mind saying things that were hurtful to the feelings of his listeners; he was indifferent to the fact that his denunciation of gurus and their systems of meditation was offending the religious susceptibilities of devout followers; he talked like a man who was possessed by a superior power of understanding which was lacking in others; his face looked grave while he spoke, which was usually in a slow and dignified way; the serious expression embodied in his face harmonised with the wise sayings that poured from his lips — sayings that were punctuated by short pauses, presumably because he wanted their inner meaning to sink deeply into the minds of his listeners; and seldom did he smile or laugh when delivering an address. Consequently, not a few created in their minds an image of K that did not correspond with the actual character of K. For they mistakenly jumped to the conclusion that K was a cheerless grumpy old gentleman. It is true that he looked melancholy and downcast at times, but such an expression was never permanently registered, because his face was like a kaleidoscope of constantly changing expressions, which gave us a hint of the extraordinary variety, vitality and richness of his inner life.

An elderly lady from New Zealand, who attended a series of talks in Madras, confessed that she had endured a long sea voyage "mainly for the pleasure of seeing Krishnamurti smile" His smile was certainly seraphic and it frequently disarmed many antagonists, who were determined to defeat K by arguing with him. He had only to smile and former foes of K forsook their futile fury and became his close friends. Wherever he went, that mysteriously enchanting smile of his was winning him new friends.

There are in existence a number of learned theses on the psychology of laughter. I regret not having questioned K on the psychological significance of laughter. I should have asked: Is there anything more to laughter, apart from its sometimes being a welcome relief from states of fear, anxiety, pain, suffering and the like? I had a fair idea of K's attitude to laughter after noticing how he responded to it. For instance, K once stated that because confused persons invariably act according to the dictates of their confusion, they cannot help choosing for themselves gurus who were also confused. Then the audience roared at K's comments. K waved his hands disapprovingly and said: "Please don't laugh. I am speaking to you in all seriousness." On another occasion he reprimanded a group of youngsters who laughed during one of his meetings. "You laugh," he said, "because you are reacting emotionally." Yet on a few occasions K himself laughed unrestrainedly whilst lecturing, when someone cracked a joke or because a funny incident occurred. For example, at an informal discussion meeting one morning, K was trying very hard to share with everyone present a deep truth that he had discovered. He was saying that there is a great joy in being able to observe anything exactly as it is, without the intervention of the "observer" because the "observer" always distorts observation. Speaking about himself in relation to pure observation, K said: "When I look at that tree in the garden, there is no "I" that is observing the tree. There is only the tree. There is only the thing observed without the "observer" looking at it."

"Does this mean," asked an elderly lady eagerly, "that the "observer" has got merged in the thing observed with the result that there is only the tree and nothing else? Does your body also disappear and become merged in the tree?"

"Of course it doesn't!" exclaimed K with a loud burst of laughter.

Bhikku Walpola Rahula, the eminent Buddhist scholar and author who had several discussions with K, once told me that he found a striking similarity between the Buddha's sense of humour and that of Krishnaji. Their sense of humour was fine and subtle; their humour revealed their extraordinary mental acuteness. There is a wise saying that you can gauge a man's intelligence or lack of it by the things that make him laugh.

His admirers enjoyed the sight of K laughing, especially because laughter made him look less like a deity and more like an ordinary person with human traits. His laughter ranged from a soft chuckle to an exuberant guffaw that borders on ecstasy. There were periods of continuous laughter that lasted a few minutes. Laughter lit up his face and tears welled up in his eyes. The emotional intensity which manifested itself in K's face during these periods was such that he resembled a bhakta in a trance. Needless to say, his laughter cheered up everyone around him.

I have never heard K resorting to unmentionable Anglo-Saxon four-letter expletives, although he must have been aware of their existence as a result of his reading detective stories and associating with many different types of people. Several times I heard him using discreet expletives, such as 'bloody' and 'damn', but nowadays who is shocked by such words? There was not the slightest hint of vulgarity, obcenity or scatology in his pure sense of humour. His humour was unblemished in the sense that it was not sardonic. He never laughed maliciously nor in a mocking manner with the intention of humiliating an opponent. He simply laughed in a childlike way at all things that are funny and ridiculous.

When a powerful politician is much disliked he soon becomes the favourite butt of our jokes. Do we not derive a subtle sadistic pleasure by thus making someone the laughingstock of society? As a general rule, we thoroughly relish laughing at others but do we ever laugh at ourselves? Are the proud ones ready to laugh at themselves and risk the probability of injuring their inflated egos? Only the truly humble ones are capable of looking inwards and then laughing at themselves. K had a great capacity to laugh at himself.

Although K's name had become a very prestigious one in the world, even during the days of his boyhood, it is noteworthy that he was not attached to it in the least. He forcefully upbraided people for worshipping his name because any kind of personal adoration, which is centred around a name, prevents their approaching the teachings afresh. Our difficulty is that we cannot easily dissociate his name from his teachings. At a private meeting he told us very clearly: "These are not my teachings but the teachings of life." This statement probably means that the teachings are precious and true, not because K happened to give expression to them, but because they are true anyway. The teachings, in other words, are intrinsically true, regardless of whether it was K or someone else who gave utterance to them. K just happened to be the exponent of certain self-evident universal truths but apparently K never wanted to have a proprietorial interest in what he taught. Therefore, is it not unfortunate that the universal teachings got linked up with a particular name? One can well understand why K laughingly remarked that he had considered changing his name from Krishnamurti to Christopher Murphy!

Those who had the pleasure of associating with K were sometimes entertained with many amusing stories, jokes and a wealth of anecdotes. K never claimed to be the author of the funny things he told us. Actually the source of some of his tales are traceable to Zen literature. The tales were somewhat modified by him. He used the jokes and stories of others to instruct and awaken all who sought his advice as well as to elucidate difficult points in the teachings. In Colombo K was seen reading a jokebook during his leisure hours. K loved the humour of Mark Twain and I noticed several books by this great American humourist in K's small personal library at Arya Vihar in Ojai, California. Some of his stories had no basis in fact but that did not matter because their purpose was to convey a message.

K enjoyed relating stories which portrayed personal behaviour that was incongruous with avowed moral principles. A good example of this type of story is the following one:

Two monks, who had taken a vow of absolute sexual abstinence — total abstinence in thought, word and deed — were slowly returning to their monastery after attending a funeral. The senior monk was walking slightly ahead of the young novice, who was carrying a small leather purse which contained all the coins that had been offered them for conducting the funeral service. As they passed the village brothel, the young novice said excitedly: "Shall we visit the local prostitute and use up all the money we earned?"

Very shocked and disgusted, the senior monk took the young novice to task: "Shame! Don't you know that you should not think such thoughts? Besides, we haven't got enough money to pay her."

The next story is also about two monks who had taken a vow relating to the strict observance of sexual purity in thought, word and deed. Together they were going on a long journey, which entailed walking for many miles through thick forests and marshy land. They were about to cross a river with a strong current, when an attractive young woman appeared on the scene and requested that she be taken across the water. "Go away, " shouted the young monk, "because we have vowed never to have any dealings with a woman."

"Please help me," she tearfully begged.

Thereupon the older monk spontaneously lifted the woman and waded across the swiftly flowing river. After crossing the stream, she thanked him for the favour and she soon left them. After this incident was over, for several days the young monk continually criticised the conduct of the older monk. The young monk angrily complained: "You behaved improperly by touching the body of a woman."

The older monk retorted: "I left the woman on the river bank but you are still carrying her!"

This story illustrates the unchaste mind of the young monk, who continued to be disturbed by an innocently performed deed that belonged to the dead past. According to K, genuine chastity consists in the freedom from all image making and image storing in the mind. His view of chastity was therefore a far cry from the traditional attitude to chastity which insisted on the avoidance of any contact with the opposite sex.

While K and I were lunching in Gstaad, Switzerland, he was curious to know the places of cultural interest I had visited during my summer holidays in Rome. I said that the highlight of my tour was a day spent browsing the shelves of the marvellous library of the Vatican, which is called Biblioteca Apostolica Vaticana. I was enthusiastically describing the ancient manuscripts, early printed books and other treasures that belong to this institution. I informed K that the administrators of this great library had gratefully accepted a gift of certain books I had written relating to his teachings. Some of his own books were also presented and very thankfully received. "It will be such fun," I said, "to question their beliefs and dogmas and shake the very foundations of the Roman Catholic Church. Don't you think it necessary to stimulate theologians into reading books relating to your teachings?"

K asked: "Are they really interested?"

I replied: "Well, we must get them interested in the teachings. Do you think the Pope would be interested in attending your talks?" The naivety of this question surprised him. With an incredulous look he said: "The Pope at Saanen? I can't see that happening." Next, K spoke about the magnificent works of art he had seen at the Vatican. I got the impression that K never had an audience with any Pope but he referred to how the smiling Pope John Paul I had greeted him by waving his hand. K showed a liking for this particular Pope, whom he described as "a friendly fellow". K regretted that he had suddenly died after a brief reign.

With considerable mirth, K told a tale:

A beggar in rags was found worshipping in the sacred Sistine Chapel, the chapel of the Pope, which is decorated with frescoes by Michelangelo and others. The beggar's presence there was immediately noticed by the Pope. Thereupon the Pope expressed his annoyance: "Who is that man kneeling there? He is not even properly dressed." The Pope ordered the beggar to leave the Sistine Chapel at once. The Pope's command had to be obeyed of course. Dejected because he was rejected by the Pope, which the devout beggar believed almost amounted to a minor excommunication from the holy Roman Catholic Church, he returned to his squalid room in a slum district of Rome. There in the privacy and silence of his room he knelt down to pray. Suddenly God appeared in person before him. The poor man could hardly believe his eyes when he saw the Almighty in all His splendour. God then lovingly spoke with the beggar and inquired of him thus:

"Sir, what is your problem?"

"My problem," he answered, "is that I was expelled from the Vatican."

"Don't worry," said God, "because even I have been expelled from the Vatican."

K was fond of jokes and anecdotes concerning Jesus and especially missionaries, who travel to distant lands with the intention of converting to Christianity the heathen who refuse to acknowledge the God of the Bible.

One of his favourite stories was about a zealous missionary who tried to preach the gospel to a group of cannibals. The cannibals were so angry with the supercilious attitude of the missionary to them that they decided to kill him and enjoy his flesh for their dinner. They were about to fry the missionary in a cauldron of boiling oil.

"Please don't eat me," begged the frightened missionary.

"What one eats," philosophized one of the cannibals, "is all a matter of taste. You love eating beefsteak but we prefer missionaries."

Some of the people who attended K's meetings were strange indeed. A bearded and long-haired young man, wearing a flowing white dress that resembled a cassock, introduced himself to K after one of his talks. "My name," he declared, "is Jesus Christ. I am the genuine Jesus. The bogus Jesus who used my name long ago was rightly crucified."

K beamed and they shook hands. After greeting this man, K said: "It is so nice to meet you Mr. Jesus Christ."

Some of us who overheard this conversation laughed heartily. This man was rather offended that his claim to be the real Jesus had made him the laughingstock of certain bystanders. He fell into a rage and stared into our eyes and walked away immediately without uttering a word.

Throughout his life K spoke emphatically against spiritual organizations. They are valueless because no organization, however well-intended and efficient, can possibly be of assistance in this inward journey of watching the thought process; moreover, involvement in the activities of spiritual organizations often becomes an escape from the all-important work of self-observation. K always maintained that Truth, which is an unapproachable 'pathless land', cannot and should not be organized. He denounced spiritual organisations by referring to the conversation between the Devil and his friend.

When the Devil and his friend were walking, they noticed a man pick up something and put it away in his pocket.

The friend: What did he pick up?

The Devil: It was a piece of Truth.

The friend: Then, isn't that bad business for you?

The Devil: Not at all because I'm going to let him organize the piece of Truth he picked up.

"A certain European writer," I informed K, "has something new and interesting to say about your origin. His occult investigations have revealed that you were not only born in another planet but also that you travelled in a spaceship to Earth. He argues that that is why you are such a hopeless misfit in this world of ambition and competition."

K laughed for awhile and asked: "Is he saying that my father did not produce me? My poor father!"

He stopped laughing and then his tired face looked very serious. K then said: "Beware of theories. Theories are binding and blinding."

K's simple and uncomplicated mind was so perceptive that he never failed to notice the incongruous and funny side of a situation. For instance, he described how many armed policemen had been entrusted with the task of safeguarding Mrs. Indira Gandhi, the Indian Prime Minister, when she once visited him in India. K then laughingly spoke about a very fat policeman who was hiding behind a very thin tree, totally unaware that he could be seen from all directions.

K laughed heartily when he was informed that a certain lady had refused to watch a film of himself giving a talk. This lady had argued that in a film K will not be able to notice the fact that she was seated in the audience and listening to him! Did K laugh at this lady's hidden vanity or her strange expectation that those seen by him were somehow going to be mysteriously benefitted?

Situated in the picturesque and hilly town of Kandy, the ancient Temple of the Tooth is widely regarded as the sanctum sanctorum of Sri Lanka for within its sacred precincts is preserved a tooth of the Buddha. Although Buddhist doctrine strictly frowns upon any kind of worship, this particular religious relic has been worshipped for centuries by devout Buddhists. Various Buddhist kings adhered to the belief that any sovereign, whose good fortune it was to possess this tooth, was somehow incapable of being conquered. When K was staying in Colombo, a Buddhist monk called on him and started praising the occult powers of this tooth. The monk audaciously instructed K: "Now that you are here, you must go to this hallowed shrine. There you must pay your respects to the tooth of Lord Buddha by offering it flowers and incense."

K laughed at the suggestion and asked: "Sir, are you sure this isn't the tooth of a crocodile?"

Dr. Kewal Motwani, sociologist and author, was

residing in Colombo when K visited that city in 1957. Dr. Motwani was an old friend of K. Long before the subcontinent had been partitioned into India and Pakistan, K had stayed with Dr. Motwani in Karachi. After partition, K intended delivering lectures in Pakistan but Dr. Motwani prevailed upon K to cancel his programme. He implored K not to go there : "Krishnaji, once they know your views, Muslim fanatics may want to kill you." K heeded his warning and no talks were given there. Consequently K was virtually unknown in the Muslim world; incidentally, he was also hardly known in the communist world.

There was an evening reception in honour of K at Dr. Motwani's mansion in Colombo. It was attended by cabinet ministers, politicians, journalists, academics and several prominent citizens. K warmly hugged Dr. Motwani, when he arrived at the latter's residence. It was a moving gesture of friendship and affection. After K had taken his seat, Dr. Motwani made a formal speech in which he welcomed K and added: "Krishnaji, whenever I am with you I feel that I am in the holy presence of the Buddha." K smiled and suddenly asked: "But have you ever been in his presence?" The absolute egolessness of K was especially evident during the aforementioned social gathering. Strange are the ways of the ego which has an unquenchable thirst for compliments. One of the remarkable characteristics of K was that he remained completely unaffected by the fact that his admirers held him in esteem. He was totally untouched by both praise and blame. When you know yourself thoroughly, does it matter what the world thinks of you?

Advice on Health

Throughout his long life, K unfailingly took the utmost care of his health. He was very concerned about maintaining his body in a fit enough condition to fulfil his mission in life — proclaiming the truth and dispelling the darkness of ignorance. A criticism often levelled against K was that he was excessively interested in his physical well-being. But what his critics failed to realize was that K needed a good strong constitution, which was capable of withstanding the strain and stress of travelling back and forth every year to India, Europe and America for the purpose of giving talks. Even when he was a doddering nonagenarian, when many of his age would rather slumber in an armchair than deliver discourses, K was still very active. It was not that he took pride or pleasure in maintaining a fine body: on the contrary, he regarded good health as a sine qua non for the continuation of his work.

K's attitude to health may also have been influenced by several other secondary factors. Given his Brahminical background with its emphasis on the highest standards of personal hygiene and proper diet, it was unlikely that K would ever have wanted to neglect his body. Conscious of the need to protect the delicate body of the boy K, Bishop C.W. Leadbeater took measures to train and strengthen it. The boy, for instance, was encouraged to swim and exercise himself.

Even at the tender age of fifteen, K wrote about the importance of looking after the body in his first classic, a little book of instructions called *At the Feet of the Master*. The body was likened to an animal — the horse upon which one rides. For this reason one should treat it well, and take good care of it; one should not overwork it, and one should feed it properly on pure food and drink only. The body, besides, must be kept clean always, "even from the minutest speck of dirt."

Hatha Yoga

One morning some of us were having a pleasant chat in the lounge of the Jawatta Road house in Colombo. K called us into his room and volunteered interesting pieces of information on hatha yoga. He instructed us in the best way of performing certain asanas. We considered ourselves doubly privileged because we had the benefit of witnessing a demonstration of several important asanas by K, who had been practising them for many years. Seeing K exercise himself was a sheer delight. Dressed only in a crumpled white pyjama, his slim and lithe body moved with the quick and graceful agility of a snake.

"Please understand," K explained, "that I am doing yoga purely for physical reasons. It is only a means of keeping fit. Yoga is a means to an end and not an end in itself. It is necessary to understand this clearly because yogis perform yoga with the intention of acquiring psychic powers or awakening the kundalini and all that stuff. Such things don't interest me."

K wide opened the windows of his room and inhaled, retained and exhaled the cool fresh morning air, when performing a series of breathing exercises that lasted for about fifteen minutes. "Pranayama exercises," he said, "are very important because they introduce oxygen into the system. The brain cannot function without oxygen. Learn to breathe correctly so that your brain is at its highest level of efficiency."

"Will pranayama exercises help me to become more intelligent?" I asked.

"Not necessarily. That's a big subject. We won't go into that now, if you don't mind," he said.

K stressed the importance of having a good sitting and standing posture. He confirmed the traditional view that having the head and spine in an upright position is conducive to the good health of the brain.

K told us that one of the many meanings of the word 'yoga' is 'skill in action'. In the realm of hatha yoga, 'skill in action' means perfectly carrying out that combination of exercises which are most suitable to the particular needs of a person.

K first learnt hatha yoga by reading a book on that subject but unfortunately he could not remember the name of its author nor title. He liked to keep on supplementing his knowledge of this vast field by learning from whomsoever was conversant with it.

After doing a succession of spinal exercises, K rested for a considerable time in the supine corpse posture (savasana). Next he spoke enthusiastically about his favourite asana, the posture of the entire body or all the limbs (sarvangasana). We did not actually see him in this posture but he described the right way of doing it and its special advantages. One has to lie flat on the back and slowly lift off the legs so that the trunk, hips and legs are all vertical. The elbows rest on the ground and the back is supported by the hands. The chin is pressed against the chest. The whole weight of the body is borne by the shoulders. Since this asana regulates the secretion of the thyroids, the most important glands of the endocrine system, the entire body is naturally benefited from doing it. It facilitates a physical regeneration.

Speaking in a light vein, K related a story which sought to explain the origin of hatha yoga. There once existed a special plant called soma in ancient India. It was considered to be of divine origin and soma juice was offered to the gods in Vedic times. This plant had a certain life-giving quality in the sense that the minds of those who consumed it became extraordinarily alert and sensitive. The wonder plant made the mind intensely sharp with the result that there was understandably a great demand for it. Soma, alas, soon became extinct and those who had once treasured it were now very distressed. That was the reason why the rishis substituted the elaborate system of hatha yoga for soma. They maintained that hatha yoga is as equally capable of awakening consciousness as soma itself.

Several years later when I met K in London, he wanted me to attend Mr. B.K.S. Iyengar's hatha yoga classes there. After attending two sessions of hatha yoga, I reported back that I much disliked the rigorous methods of Mr. Iyengar, who often forced his students to do certain difficult postures when their bodies were still unprepared for them. An asana, I argued, is surely a comfortable posture of ease and relaxation that is conducive to meditation, something that is done slowly and effortlessly; but this teacher, perhaps because he wanted his students to progress quickly, was ignoring the fact that the body requires a long period of adjustment before it becomes supple enough to do complicated corporeal contortions. I referred to the possible deleterious effects of compelling the body to do exercises. One should treat the body gently instead of roughly and violently. K heartily endorsed my opinion on this subject and informed me that he had himself already stopped following the Iyengar system.

Food Without Cruelty

Many ethical, philosophical, economic and nutritional arguments can be adduced in support of vegetarianism. Nowadays many avoid the consumption of fish, flesh and fowl because they subscribe to the doctrine of non-injury (ahimsa) or some such religious principle that forbids killing. But K did not subscribe to any belief nor ideology. K's lifelong adherence to vegetarianism was not the outcome of cold reasoning. His vegetarianism was born in the womb of compassion. His compassion for animals equalled his great compassion for human beings. The infliction of any kind of pain or injury on any living creature was absolutely abhorrent to his nature. He deeply loved and respected all animals: the tame pets as well as the dangerous wild animals that he accidentally saw during the course of his solitary walks in forests. His books have references to some of his non-verbal communications with animals.

A friend of mine who lives in England was softly admonished by K thus: "Sir, I know from your breath that you eat meat. Don't eat it. It is poison!" I do not know whether this person's feelings were hurt after hearing such words. In K's role as an itinerant spiritual teacher, there were numerous occasions when he inevitably had to make remarks of this kind, which questioned the settled dietary habits of people and consequently disturbed their peace of mind.

In *At the Feet of the Master*, K denounced the awful slaughter of animals that was necessitated by the superstition that required the sacrificing of animals. He also referred to "the still more cruel superstition that man needs flesh for food."

When I informed K that the vast majority of Buddhist monks in Sri Lanka unashamedly ate meat and fish and justified their actions by quoting sacred books, he was very saddened. "Poor Buddha!" K exclaimed.

In 1974 I resigned from my position in the British Library because of my new appointment in Adelaide, where I was Librarian of the South Australian Parliamentary Library for twelve years (1974-86). Before my departure from England, I visited K and said goodbye. K looked at me intensely and said: "Change your environment if you must, but what is far more urgent is bringing about a complete change within yourself." He disapproved of my plan to live in Australia. His parting advice was: "Wherever you may go, don't waste your life." Was it a waste of one's life, I wondered, to go to a new country and accept a more lucrative job? Had not K himself been to Australia several times to give talks?

My Australian salary was so high that I could easily afford to travel overseas several times a year to listen to K's talks in faraway places like America, England, Switzerland and India. During the last decade of K's life, I was especially lucky because I met K several times every year in different parts of the world. Whenever he happened to see me, the first question he asked was either "Do you really like Australia?" or "When are you going to leave Australia?" But it was only in the summer of 1981, while we were lunching together at Chalet Tannegg (Gstaad, Switzerland), that I fully understood why he objected to the

Australian way of life. "In Australia," complained K, "they eat chunks of meat that are nicely hidden between slices of bread. How can you live in a country like that? Do you want to become one of them?"

On one occasion K was asked whether the freedom from such vices as the use of alcohol, tobacco and non-vegetarian foods was likely to help one in understanding his teachings. His answer was simple: It is not what one puts into the mouth that gives one understanding! One is not going to understand reality merely by giving up these things. It is by discovering the limitations of the mind and heart, and transcending them, that one comes by liberation.

If a man "gives up" eating meat in the expectation of spiritual advancement, is he acting out of genuine sympathetic concern for the suffering of animals? Is he not acting out of sheer self-concern? In this case, is it not the ambitious self that is trying to expand itself under the respectable guise of spirituality? One can of course become a vegetarian for a million reasons but only that kind of vegetarianism is sublime which is inspired by selfless compassion.

Right Nutrition

"If you care for the welfare of your body," observed K, "you would read and find out what the experts have said about right nutrition. Vegetarianism in itself will not automatically ensure good health because you should take only nutritious vegetarian food and avoid anything that upsets the system. In my life I have always given importance to two things — being alone and taking the right food."

K ate very little and every item of food that entered his mouth was thoroughly masticated. A busy businessman, who was given to gobbling his meals, was advised by K: "Chew and chew and chew again and then drink down your food." In the dining hall K ate so slowly that he was invariably the last person to finish eating.

Lunch was his main meal for the day. He began by eating a fruit such as an apple or a mango. This was followed by raw uncooked food, which was usually a salad. The next course consisted of cooked food such as a savoury or boiled rice. He ended the meal with a wholemeal biscuit or a small piece of Lindt chocolate from Switzerland. Lindt is reputedly the best kind of chocolate in the world. Incidentally, several times I had the pleasure of presenting K with boxes of Lindt chocolates. I noticed that he liked to select the tiniest piece of chocolate for himself and distribute the rest to whomsoever happened to be near him. He was devoid of any sense of ownership and he loved to share or give away whatever he was given.

During the evening of K's life he was interested in taking ginseng to recover his health and overcome tiredness. From time to time I sent him supplies of ginseng and fresh cheese which he much appreciated.

Understanding the Nature of Disease

K maintained that understanding the causes of an illness is more helpful than trying to overcome it. Our minds are so accustomed to pursuing pleasures and pushing aside pains that we are reluctant to live with an illness. Instead of remaining with an illness we desire to get rid of it as soon as possible. A fever, for example, is a blessing in disguise because it burns harmful toxins and thereby purifies the body.

When K was asked whether he supported allopathy, homeopathy, naturopathy or any other system of treating diseases, he answered the question non-committally by saying: "I suppose there is some truth in each system."

"Every morsel of food that enters your stomach," observed K, "is directly or indirectly going to influence your health. Therefore, mustn't you watch very carefully your reactions to different kinds of foods and medicines?" K also advised me that there is a close relationship between physical exercise and what he called 'the intelligence of the body': "Sir, are you destroying the natural intelligence of the body by too little exercise or too much exercise? Try to avoid both extremes. Find out also whether your daily activities are making you too tired and weakening your resistance to disease."

One of my difficulties is that any kind of sickness lowers my spirits. When illness enters through the door, cheerfulness disappears through the window. K was specifically questioned whether physical indispositions caused within himself any feeling of depression. K made it clear that although he had suffered from various illnesses during his life none of these had ever affected his inward state of being.

The Art of Relaxation

In spite of the fact that K never had the advantage of a formal medical education, his intuitive understanding of the body was very deep. One of my many interviews with K was mostly devoted to a discussion on the art of relaxation. "Before we discuss relaxation, have you cared to find out for yourself the reasons that are making you tense?" he said. He pointed out that any worry or problem would be in the way of total relaxation. He also indicated that even drinking tea and coffee is one of the factors that prevents relaxation. "When your body is tired," he suggested, "don't take any stimulants. All you then need is a period of quietness."

It was a hot afternoon and nearly everyone present in the hall was perspiring. K was particularly exhausted from more than an hour of uninterrupted talking and answering written questions. "Please may I take a breather?" he requested in a faint voice. He immediately closed his eyes and remained so for about five minutes. He was seated cross-legged on the ground. His entire body was motionless and his face radiated an ineffable tranquillity. How like a classical Buddha statue he looked! When he suddenly opened his eyes he had a countenance which was both fresh and vivacious. He smiled and asked: "Can you also rest like that?" K explained the essence of right relaxation:

"When your mind is absolutely still a new energy comes from outside and regenerates you."

How the Sick were Healed

K was reticent about his reputed ability to heal people of their physical illnesses. Yet there were occasions when he casually referred to various persons who at some time or other had been healed by him. As far as possible, he carefully tried to avoid using the word 'heal': he preferred the expression 'I helped'.

The details of how K healed Vimala Thakar of her ear ailment are well known because they have been vividly described in her book titled *On an Eternal Voyage* (1966). After the publication of this work, many sick persons visited K and humbly begged for his help. There were the chronic sufferers who particularly sought his assistance. The sick and the dying came with demands for compassionate consideration and care of their complaints. One can sympathise with the longing of diseased persons to find lasting solutions to their physical problems, especially in situations where the usual methods of treatment failed to produce satisfactory results. K seemed embarrassed that numerous patients were approaching him, and requesting that he should somehow restore them to sound health. K told them frankly but kindly: "Please, I am not a doctor." He advised them thus: "Go and consult a medical expert." Needless to say, many patients were disappointed in K. Once when K refused to treat a French lady of a certain bodily condition, she quickly cited the case of Vimala Thakar. She argued that Vimala had enjoyed preferential treatment merely because of her Indian origins. She proceeded to scold K, and angrily accused him of 'practising racial discrimination' because K was himself a person of Indian birth. Surprised by her fury and also slightly amused, K exclaimed: "Good Lord!" It is definitely incorrect that K had racist tendencies. He loved all human beings alike — men, women and especially children, from all countries. A person's social class, race or colour never coloured his outlook. It should be mentioned in passing that several persons of European origin were also healed by him. A few instances of such healing will be mentioned later in this discussion.

There were times when K eagerly wanted to heal suffering individuals; but when he tried to do so, his efforts were either totally unsuccessful or only partially successful. The reason why he did not have a success rate of one-hundred percent is difficult to understand. Another matter that is beyond one's comprehension is why he sometimes turned down pleas for help from people who were in great physical pain. Was he acting callously? Behaviour that was indifferent to the suffering of others was so much out of character. Perhaps he subscribed to the view that certain illnesses should not be arrested because of their beneficial effect of purifying and regenerating the whole system.

I have been puzzled by the fact that K, whose life was full of many minor illnesses and several major ones as well as fatal cancer, was apparently lacking in the ability to heal himself of them. Was K deficient in the power to heal himself of physical disorders? Could it not have been the case that he actually had the power to heal himself but was unwilling to exercise it? One can speculate about this question endlessly and still remain in the dark.

"Man, heal thyself" is a doctrine that is nicely compatible with the teachings of K, but only insofar as psychological matters are concerned; however, regarding non-psychological situations, such as when one is physically unwell, then not seeking any external assistance, such as that of an healer, may be the height of folly, especially if healing is the only known means of effecting a permanent cure.

"I didn't do it! I didn't do *anything!*" These were the emphatic words of K, when he was informed that he had healed a certain person of a very serious illness. Obviously he was refusing to take any credit for this person's sudden restoration of health. Whereas in the past he had readily admitted that he 'helped' in the healing process, on this occasion he was disclaiming all responsibility for it.

Toward the latter part of his life, K maintained that he was only an instrument of healing. His mind-heart was so pure and fine that some indescribable power, 'the otherness', was using him to effect miraculous cures. It was as though Mother Nature was channelling her restorative, regenerative and curative qualities through K, who was himself a perfect child of Nature. K's role in the healing process could be likened to that of a typewriter that is used by a typist. The typewriter is incapable of typing anything of its own accord. The typewriter, in other words, is a mere docile instrument or medium in the hands of the typist.

Those who were receptive and sensitive to it, the few lucky ones, were able to tap that hidden power and energy which flowed through K. Sometimes, persons who were in close physical proximity to him became the beneficiaries of that mysterious energy which manifested itself in K. Now let us consider a good example of this kind of healing. A deeply agitated Tamil gentleman from Jaffna, whose lips were trembling with anxiety, visited Ackland House in Colombo, when K was residing there in 1980. He brought along his four-year old epileptic son. The boy was also suffering from a speech defect with the result that articulating distinctly had become impossible. The child had a sickly complexion. This man requested me to arrange for him a meeting with K as he was desirous of getting his son healed soon. Acting on behalf of this person, I explored the possibility of organising such a meeting. I was told that K was not granting any more private interviews because he was feeling very tired. When this message was conveyed to the father of the child, he insisted that he should not be denied the opportunity to meet K. He begged tearfully: "Allow us only five minutes to be with Krishnaji." His request for a meeting was turned down for the second time. Thereupon I tried to console him by suggesting that the child should be brought to K's public talks. "Go early to the hall," I advised him, "and sit in a place that is nearest to the platform from where K speaks." He accepted the idea. The man and child regularly attended all the talks and were seen seated on the ground right in front of K. At the end of the series of talks, this person turned up at Ackland House with a basketful of the best Jaffna mangoes, which were all ripe and fresh. It was a present for K. The man looked very cheerful and relaxed. He smilingly told me that his son, who attended all the talks but could not have understood them because he was ignorant of English, no longer suffered from epilepsy. As for the speech defect, this also had strangely disappeared.

It has long been believed that the effectiveness of healing depends on the magic touch of the healer's hands. The example already considered involved neither touching nor stroking. K, the healer, did not even know that he was involved in the healing. It is necessary to reiterate that the evidence relating to K's acts of healing is strongly suggestive that the ultimate source or origin of his healing power cannot be traced to himself. K was merely the means whereby an extraordinary force was transmitted to others for their benefit. This force was probably outside the conscious control of K himself, in the sense that it was not something that operated at his behest.

K liked to belittle his acts of healing. At a discussion meeting K recounted an experience he had when he was young. K was going for a walk in a medieval Dutch city when a leper, who had been waiting for K in a narrow street, came forward and made a grab at K's body. As a result of that physical contact the leper was totally healed of his condition. A few days later, this person did "something wrong" (K did not specify the wrongdoing), and consequently he was imprisoned. K posed the question: "Did I really help that man? Anyone can heal the body but you alone can heal your mind. The state of your mind affects the state of your health. So it is far more important to clear up the mess inside and bring about order in the mind." Right behaviour is something that K expected of those who are seriously interested in his teachings. Had this man taken the trouble to disentangle his mind from anti-social traits, would he not have behaved properly?

At the picturesque Alpine village of Saanen in Switzerland, K spoke continually for twenty-five years. It was there that I regularly met a well-dressed European gentleman, who was always conspicuous in the crowd of listeners because he was given to wearing a trilby hat. He usually sat alone on the last row of seats. Rarely did he speak with any of those who attended these meetings. He confessed that he was "not particularly interested in hearing these lectures." I asked him the obvious question: "Then why do you come here?" I am glad that I made notes of the interesting explanation he gave:

"I come to Saanen to express my gratitude to

Krishnamurti — the saviour of my life. I like seeing him. Seeing this man of dignified bearing is like taking a tonic. The main reason why I come here is because forty-five years ago I was suffering from consumption. In the olden days 'consumption' was the name given to 'tuberculosis'. One of my lungs was so badly damaged that the doctors wanted to remove it. One afternoon I visited Krishnamurti without making a prior appointment. You see, I wanted to get his advice about whether to have an operation. He was walking out of the gates. He said: "Please excuse me. I've had a busy day and I'm too tired to meet you. I'm going for a stroll. You may accompany me if you wish." I agreed. So we walked together for a long time through meadows and fields and he hardly spoke. When we were standing on a bare stretch of land, Krishnamurti said: "The moment I saw you I recognised your illness. My brother had the same trouble." He then asked me not to feel any fear: "Don't be scared." The next thing that happened was that his fingers started running over my vertebral column. He rubbed my spine with his hands. I felt an upsurge of heat that started moving in the direction of my head. I felt a burning sensation in the upper part of the body. There was an uneasy heaviness and I was about to collapse. He held me firmly and helped me to walk back to his house. A few weeks later I felt stronger in body and my health definitely improved. Tests were carried out and the doctors pronounced that the diseased lung was no longer diseased. There was no need for an operation."

There is a certain writer who is personally known to me. He regularly used to attend K's talks in Bombay and Madras. He is tall, slim and strong. He never had a major illness in his life. Quite unexpectedly, he began losing weight and feeling extremely tired. He was shocked when he heard several medical experts state that his life expectancy was going to be very short because of a cancerous growth in his mouth. He philosophically resigned himself to the inevitability of his forthcoming death. By means of a will, he left his property to his children. His next important act was to call on K for the last time. During the course of their conversation, K asked him to open his mouth widely as he wanted to see for himself this malignant growth, instead of relying on medical opinion. According to this gentleman, K looked into his mouth in the manner of a dentist. K gently touched his throat and said: "Don't worry. You will be all right." About a week later, the doctors were surprised that the cancer had ceased to exist. It was seven years ago that he was healed, and I am pleased to report that the cancer has so far not recurred anywhere in his body.

During the late evenings, when the birds are returning to their resting places for the night, K loved to haunt the lovely sandy stretch of beach that borders the estate of the Theosophical Society at Adyar in Madras. Accompanied by the society's President, Radha Burnier and other friends, K enjoyed walking from the bridge that spans the muddy Adyar River to a nearby place along the shore, where there is a cluster of shacks, which are the homes of fishermen and their families. Sometimes children from the slums, poverty-stricken and dressed in rags, would follow K or surround him in a curious manner. He did not avoid them as some snobbish rich persons are wont to do. Once I saw K affectionately patting these children on their heads. It was a delight to see K walking fast with his long arms swinging in the cool evening breeze. Now and again he stopped walking, and gazed with joy at the choppy sea and the distant horizon. His walks were frequently interrupted by passers-by, who either engaged in brief conversations with K or exchanged friendly greetings with him. Indians and people from far distant lands, who had come for the talks, gathered here in large numbers at sunset. K was naturally the cynosure of all eyes.

One pleasant evening, an Indian friend and I were comfortably seated on a sand ridge. Needless to say, we were awaiting the arrival of K on the beach. Regarded by many as a sacred place, it was here that Bishop Leadbeater first noticed the boy K whose aura, he said, was devoid of selfishness. My friend, who is deeply interested in K's teachings, was discussing her personal problems. She is well-to-do and healthy, except for her frequent attacks of migraine. It is a disease that caused her great misery because of the severe headaches, nausea and vomiting. She spent a fortune trying to cure herself. For years she tried different kinds of treatment but all her efforts to find a solution to this problem were fruitless. I taught her a few yogic breathing exercises, which she practised, but there was no significant improvement in her condition.

As we were talking, we saw the slim silhouette of K in the distance. He was quickly walking towards us. Possessed by a strange emotion, she exclaimed: "I want to kiss his hands! Shall I do it?"

I replied: "You are free to do what you like."

She ran and held K's hands. Then she kissed them.

This meeting only lasted a few seconds.

After that incident she has never again been tormented with migraine.

One of the scenic attractions of Colombo is a famous sea front called Galle Face Green, where K was fond of walking leisurely in the evenings. It had been a racecourse in times past and a venue for political meetings and military parades. Today it is primarily used by persons who wish to relax and enjoy the fresh sea-breeze. K and I were walking there one evening in November 1980. During the hour we spent together several noteworthy things happened.

K saluted the stormy bluish green sea by respectfully bowing before it. He also bowed four times by turning northwards, southwards, eastwards and westwards. It was as though he were solemnly performing some ancient mystical ceremony. I suppose that was his way of marvelling at the infinite vastness of space and the beauty of nature. The multicoloured sky is enchantingly beautiful immediately before the sun sets and soon afterwards.

K found a fairly large stone on the middle of the footpath along which we were walking. It was an object that could easily have caused an unwary person to stumble and fall. K tried to lift the stone but it was too heavy for him. Next he pushed it away forcefully with his foot and thereby cleared the footpath. Many such public-spirited acts of his remain unknown because he seldom referred to them.

Two young men recognised K. They immediately greeted him and said: "Sir, you don't know us. But we know a lot about you." K shrugged his shoulders and quickly moved away from them. It struck me then that one of the disadvantages of being famous is that society rarely respects a celebrity's right to privacy.

K was walking briskly and at the same time gazing skywards and admiring the colour and shape of a dark cloud with a silver border, when a middle-aged couple, raised their arms and stopped him. We found ourselves facing a dark stout Sinhalese lady, who was dressed in a white sari. She was accompanied by her bespectacled husband. First she greeted K and apologetically said: "Excuse me for disturbing you. Please can you do me a favour?"

K waved his hand sideways in a gesture of reluctance and said: "I'm going for a walk now."

The lady tried to dissuade K from proceeding with his walk by saying: "It won't take long. Do me the favour of touching my ear — just once. From birth I've been deaf in one ear. Can you cure me?"

K declined to touch her. He simply said: "I'm sorry."

The lady started sobbing. Disappointed and irritated, her husband criticised K in a stern voice: "We have heard that you have cured other people. Why can't you cure my wife? Do you only heal your favourites?"

K stated that he wished to remain undisturbed that evening. I wondered what exactly he meant by that statement. Probably he was trying to convey a message that he did not like meeting people that evening for an undisclosed reason. Well, if the peacefulness of solitude is what he wished to have, then one must not expect to find it in a public place that is traversed by thousands.

K wanted to go away, but he was prevented from doing so, because the lady was tightly holding K's left arm! She repeatedly pleaded for his help.

K said: "Oh, no. I'm sorry, madam."

Sometimes it is very difficult to understand why K acted in a certain way. Although he was the personification of love, often in the minds of strangers the mistaken impression was formed that K was a person with a rough temper who also lacked compassion.

As I commisserated with the unhappiness of this lady, I spoke with K about my idea of the best course of action to be taken under the circumstances.

I said: "Sir, she is only asking you to touch her deaf ear. Unless you do that they will not allow you to move away from here."

K whispered: "All right then."

K hurriedly touched her on the deaf ear. Thereafter he stroked her head in a circulatory movement with his long tapering fingers. Finally, he touched again her faulty ear. The fat lady smiled with satisfaction. She thanked him and then she released her firm grip on his arm. K was allowed to go away.

After one of K's public discourses in Colombo, I accidentally met this couple at a bus-stop. She said: "That stone-deafness has gone. I can hear a little now. Please tell Krishnaji that I am very grateful to him."

Recipe for Removing Racism

I was the victim of various acts of racial discrimination during the fourteen years that I lived in England. The virus of racism manifested itself in a thousand subtle ways. I was jeered at because of my brown complexion. I was also the butt of jokes with racist overtones. I was deliberately deprived of promotions and underpaid by several employers. K was acutely aware of my secret suffering. "Are they treating you well?" was a question which he frequently asked me. One of the many valuable things I learned from him was never to retort an insult. K counselled against taking retaliatory action: "Just observe your reaction to any unkind word and your hurt will wither away." That was K's recipe for living harmoniously in an unfriendly society.

A social worker posed the following question at a meeting in London: What is your solution to the existence of the colour bar which prevents the free association of persons of different colours?

K said: "Sir, aren't we all coloured? Isn't white also a colour?"

At a meeting in London K was discoursing on the nature of nationalism and how it was responsible for the break-up of the world into tiny fragments. An angry young man heckled K with shouts and asked a rude question: Why don't you return to India and preach to your own primitive people?

K said: "Yes, sir, truth comes only to the person whose mind is primitive in the sense of its being simple and unconditioned." K remained calm and never lost his composure despite the hostility of certain members of the public.

How Many were Fully Transformed?

Countless thousands listened to K's discourses and read his books but how many of them were fully transformed? We were all influenced by what he said with the result that minor changes took place in our lives. Many reported that there had been certain secondary changes, such as their giving up the consumption of alcohol and meat. Some became free of dependence on priests and psychiatrists for solving their personal problems. Admittedly, there were some changes but did the great change happen? By the phrase 'great change' is meant the total transformation of the mind-heart or the complete dropping away of all self-centred activity.

At K's talks I met several persons who mistakenly believed that they had become enlightened after listening to K. One such man went to the extent of copying K's hairstyle and aping his gestures. We conversed for a few minutes. His opinions revealed his confused and fragmented mind for he was fiercely nationalistic and he defended America's military role in the Vietnam War. The mind, alas, is capable of creating comforting delusions, the most grandiose of which is the belief that 'I am enlightened', as though the 'I', which is the very root of all bondage, were capable of finding Liberation.

K once laughingly referred to a man who visited him and loudly boasted that he had thoroughly unconditioned his mind and was therefore totally free. A few days later, this person became a Roman Catholic and embraced all the beliefs and dogmas of that faith! K observed that a genuinely enlightened person would never feel the need to make a public or private parade of his supposed enlightenment. An enlightened person is a light unto himself in the sense that he is not dependent on anything or anybody; he is devoid of the desire to show off his spiritual accomplishments. Speaking about himself, K remarked that he would never fail to notice the existence of that state of Liberation in any person who happened to have it.

Not being an enlightened person oneself, has one that sharpness of intelligence to distinguish a genuinely enlightened person from someone who is feigning enlightenment? Years ago a question that troubled me much was that there was no objective and reliable method of testing and determining whether someone is actually enlightened or otherwise. Such a question naturally arose in my mind because it was widely assumed that certain sages like the Buddha, Ramana Maharshi and K were enlightened.

The words and external appearance of sages can be deceptive. A very wise sage may not necessarily have a saintly disposition; conversely, a pious sage may not necessarily have a high degree of intelligence. Besides, is it not dangerous to accept the claim of a spiritual master that he has realized the Truth, even when he sincerely believes in that assertion, because he could very well be mistaken?

After rejecting all external guides on account of their untrustworthiness, is it any safer to turn to one's own intuition as a last resort? Will a flash of intuition, the so-called voice of God, help to resolve this question? Let us not overlook the fact that even intuition, like thought itself, is a product of the mind. A decision that is based on intuition, instead of being objective and impartial, will be influenced and distorted by all the hidden unconscious traits, such as one's fears, hates and prejudices. A decision founded on intuition must be open to suspicion.

I sounded Dr. Adikaram as to whether he would include K in the galaxy of enlightened sages, those rare luminaries whose lives adorn the pages of history. He thought for some time and spoke with characteristic solemnity: "I have long considered this question, going back to the 1930s when I first listened to Krishnaji. You must understand that it is given in the Buddhist scriptures that an arhat does not dream. An arhat has no residuary thought that needs to rise up in the form of a dream. For this reason a person who does not dream has to be regarded as being enlightened. That is the supreme test. So with this valuable bit of information in hand I asked Krishnaji whether he has dreams. He answered that he never dreams. Have I removed your doubt concerning Krishnaji's enlightenment?"

Is our inability to view the teachings with a fresh mind, uncontaminated by preconceived opinions of them, one of the main impediments to the radical transformation of the mind-heart? There is no freshness in our approach to the teachings in the sense that we accept only those aspects of the teachings that agree with our ideological background and reject statements by K that are psychologically disturbing. In his book titled *The Quiet Mind* (1971), John E. Coleman reported one of his conversations with K. K described a situation in which a person, who being desirous of taking shelter from the rain, walks into the tent where K is discoursing and then listens to K, about whom he has never heard before. "Perhaps in such a situation of spontaneity," observed K, "that man will understand what I am saying."

Although his audiences consisted of numerous listeners, were even a handful profoundly changed by his message? When he dissolved the Order of the Star at the Ommen Camp on August 3rd 1929, he delivered an eloquent address. Of what use, he asked, is it to have thousands with no understanding, who reject the new and translate it "to suit their own sterile, stagnant selves?" He said that it will be sufficient if there were "only five people who will listen, who will live, who have their faces turned towards eternity." In his lifetime, K may have expected to find five radically transformed human beings, but did he find at least one such person? One wonders.

Whenever my spirits were low, it was my practice to visit K, if he happened to be in town. But the experience of seeing him and spending a few quiet moments together or having a short conversation with him, these meetings seldom had the desired effect of cheering me up. In fact, when I was in a depressed state of mind, he usually said disturbing things that made me feel even more depressed. Whenever I sought the company of K with the intention of escaping from an emotional crisis, he virtually compelled me to look straightforwardly at the problem itself. He showed the futility of all escapes and the senselessness of playing with psychological toys (in the category of 'toys' he included gurus, priests, psychiatrists, churches, temples and ashrams), with the result that, at least for a while, one's undivided attention got focussed on the way the thought process operated. Like a skilled blacksmith who straightens a crooked nail by hammering it, K's questions and comments and criticisms had the effect of making the mind a piercing instrument that is capable of delving into itself.

One day I was so depressed that I visited K and blurted out that the people interested in his teachings were really getting nowhere. There was a touch of self-pity in my words: "I have resigned myself to the probability that the radical inward transformation, about which you talk so much, may never take place in me during my present lifetime. I don't know whether there is an afterlife. Perhaps I might have better luck in a future life. You have preached for so many years but hardly anyone has experienced a total mutation of the psyche. I am of course not holding you responsible for our failures. But isn't it sad and frustrating for you that all your efforts have been in vain in the sense that no one so far has found enlightenment?"

Thereupon K looked at me in a grave manner and corrected one of my statements: "Sir, it is not true that none has radically changed."

K then described two instances of psychological mutation: 'I had gone into retreat in North India amidst the lovely mountains. Everyday a sannyasin walked past the house where I was staying. We became good friends. I think he lived somewhere high up in the mountains. During the mornings he walked down the footpath to the valley and returned to his cave later. One day I questioned the sannyasin as to the reason why he was returning to the cave. He answered: "To remain silent."

He was asked: "Is there silence if your mind is chattering?" The question shocked his mind. He saw something very clearly. All chattering stopped and he was completely changed.'

With a bewitching smile, K added: "And instead of going to the cave he walked into the valley below where the people live."

In the aforementioned case, it is doubtful whether K was personally responsible for the cessation of the sannyasin's thought process. Did it not take place rather because the sannyasin himself happened to realize a great truth? Although many of us have repeatedly heard K explain that the chattering of the mind is the main obstacle to silence, why then are our wretched minds still addicted to chattering? Surely we have only ourselves to blame for our psychologically enslaved state.

K proceeded to describe the second instance of total liberation in his own words: 'After seeing off a friend at a railway station, I was returning home. A stranger asked: "Shall I walk with you?"

"You may," was my reply.

Next he lit a cigarette and was enjoying it.

"Smoking is a stupid habit," he suddenly said.

"Perhaps it is," was my reply.

The man then threw away his cigarette and trampled it. At that moment he became free not only of smoking but of all conditioning. The mind was fundamentally transformed.'

Why the Krishnamurti Bibliographies were Produced

When I was on the staff of the British National Bibliography in London, it occurred to me one day that the lack of a good K bibliography was one of the reasons why K's teachings were not as widely known as they deserved to be. At that time the teachings were the scoff of the academic world in the sense that many professors liked to ignore the existence of K's books; they hardly recommended K's works for studying and scholars were rarely encouraged to write theses on various aspects of the teachings. Therefore I wanted to compile a bibliographical key to the vast and growing literature relating to K. It was felt that a comprehensive bibliography will be useful in various institutions, especially in public libraries and universities; it will enable many persons to become aware of the extent of K's writings, if not to be introduced to his books for the first time; it will also bring to light his lesser known publications with all the treasures of wisdom they contain.

Mr. Theodore Besterman, the celebrated bibliographer and prolific writer who wrote *Mrs Annie Besant: a Modern Prophet* and *A World Bibliography of Bibliographies,* used to frequent the library of the British Museum where I worked. When I sought his advice concerning the intended bibliography, Mr. Besterman's words were a source of great encouragement to me: "The project sounds quite feasible. It will be a tremendous undertaking but something worth doing. I wish you good luck."

No sooner had I written to a few friends about the forthcoming bibliography than I started receiving avalanches of books and clippings relating to K. Masses of rare magazines, leaflets and pamphlets arrived from the far corners of the globe. The news about the bibliography had obviously spread widely because most of the donors of books were total strangers, such as the elderly Theosophist who presented her entire Krishnamurtiana collection, which she had laboriously accumulated over the years.

I was obsessed by the bibliography. It so happened that for four years all my spare time, including my annual holidays, were devoted to gathering relevant facts from various sources. I visited the national libraries of several countries and the Adyar Library and Research Centre in search of bibliographical information.

My work was progressing satisfactorily. Naturally I was in high spirits when I arrived in Paris with the intention of having a good browse through certain books in the Bibliotheque Nationale. While I was strolling the streets, I yielded to an inexplicable impulse to visit a small patisserie in Boulevard Saint Germain. It was a small shop, which sells only pastries and cakes. There I enquired whether they had any books relating to K. The young salesgirl looked at me surprisedly. She said rather impatiently: "Can't you see from our shopwindow that this is *not* a bookshop?"

I apologized to her for my mistake and was about to leave the patisserie immediately. "Wait a minute, monsieur," shouted the elderly manageress, who thereupon dashed upstairs. I waited for about twenty minutes. The manageress returned from her storeroom with a huge dusty box containing old books. She handed me the box and said: "These are all yours. I am giving them free of charge. Nobody wants them. They have been here for some twenty years or more." Great was my astonishment when I realized that this gift consisted of rare out-of-print books by K that belonged to the period before the Second World War. What a strange experience! Finding such invaluable books in such an unexpected place was indeed a minor miracle. It struck me then that probably an unseen hand was helping me and trying to further the cause of K's teachings.

I visited K immediately after I returned to England. I enthusiastically informed him that the bibliography was nearing completion. I expected him to share my eagerness but I was very upset when he disapproved of the entire project. He shrugged his shoulders and exclaimed: "What a waste of time!" He added: "Why don't you burn all the books, including my own books? Books are of no value. You will never find it in books. Writing a bibliography! Sir, self-observation is far more important." Fortunately I did not take K literally. If all the books were destroyed, would not poor librarians like myself find ourselves suddenly unemployed?

We did not see each other for nearly twelve months. Then after one of K's public talks I greeted him. K held my hand and said: "How are you keeping? When is the bibliography going to be published? Get it published soon. I'm sure it will be a very useful book." I decided to follow his instructions forthwith. I also decided not to meet K until after the actual publication of the book lest he should change his mind about its usefulness during the intervening period. That night I jotted down the following sentences in my notebook: How a conditioned mind is going to react in a given situation can be foreseen. Its reactions will be determined by the various influences that have shaped its character. But the responses of a liberated mind cannot be foreseen because it is devoid of any underlying psychological background. K's mind is as unpredictable as the English weather!

In 1974 A *Bibliography of the Life and Teachings of Jiddu Krishnamurti* was published in Leiden by E.J. Brill. It listed 1559 items. The work was warmly received in various countries and all the book reviews were commendatory. A typical book review is the one that appeared in *Codex Shambhala* vol.4 no.2. What follows is a short extract from it:

> "This excellent bibliography covers works written by Krishnamurti himself as well as those written about him. It will be a very helpful tool

for those interested in reading his works in a chronological order, thereby acquiring a feeling and an understanding of Krishnamurti's own development. The first part is devoted to Krishnamurti's own writings and is classified into Prose Works, Discourses and Discussions, Poems, Education, and Articles in Periodicals. The second part contains a listing of works about Krishnamurti, his life, and his philosophy."

A copy of the elegantly printed book was promptly posted to K and he acknowledged the gift:

2/11 A Herbert Road,
Ashford,
South Australia 5035
Australia
April 28, 1975

Dear Krishnaji,

As I now live in distant Australia I much regret not being in a position to present this book personally to you.

After several years of hard work and painstaking research it is really a great relief and joy to see the publication of *A Bibliography of the Life and Teachings of Jiddu Krishnamurti.*

There are millions in the world who, alas, have never heard of Krishnamurti. I hope this book helps in the wider dissemination of the teachings. The bibliography will be useful in libraries of various kinds throughout the world.

Krishnaji, you are a Light to the world.

I wish you good health and a very long life.

Warmest greetings,
Susunaga Weeraperuma

Brockwood Park,
Bramdean,
Nr. Alresford,
Hampshire.
S024 OLQ
17th May 1975

My dear Weeraperuma,

Thank you very much indeed for sending me your book. You must have taken infinite trouble to collect all the information. It must have taken you years.

I am sorry that you are so far away and I hope there will be some occasion when we will meet again.

With best wishes,
Yours affectionately,
Krishnamurti

It became necessary to publish the second volume of the bibliography titled *Supplement to A Bibliography of the Life and Teachings of Jiddu Krishnamurti* (Bombay: Chetana, 1982). An extract from the Preface explains why this book was published:

"The published literature on Krishnamurti is growing by leaps and bounds. It is an indication that more and more people throughout the world are becoming seriously interested in his teachings. After their long slumber of indifference to Krishnamurti, even the academic world of the universities and other institutions of higher learning are now at last awakening to his importance as evidenced by the significant number of university theses concerning various aspects of the teachings that have been successfully submitted in recent times. It is a fair guess that this prolific output of books and articles in periodicals (including non-book materials such as films, cassettes, video-cassettes and the like) will continue for a very long time. Hence there arises the need to update periodically, perhaps every few years, *A Bibliography of the Life and Teachings of Jiddu Krishnamurti* (Leiden: E.J. Brill, 1974) which attempted to cover the period up to 1972. This first supplement to the original edition is not merely a record of the publications that are known to have appeared during the last nine years (1972-1981). It also includes certain items that should have been listed in the main work published earlier."

Mr. Sudhakar S. Dikshit of Chetana must be given special credit for publishing this attractively printed Supplement.

Mr. Sudhakar S. Dikshit's Services to Krishnamurti's Teachings

During the four decades from the 1950s right until the present day, the house of Chetana has been rendering a service of inestimable value to all lovers of Truth by publishing various spiritual, religious and philosophical works, especially those books concerning the teachings of K. It is a tribute to the spiritual outlook of Mr. Dikshit that he published several important books consisting of K s own words, namely, the series of 19 volumes titled *Early Writings*, *Early Talks* and *Later Talks* comprising out-of-print valuable material reproduced in the *Chetana* monthly edited by Mr. Dikshit. He also published an anthology of quotations from K titled *Sayings of J. Krishnamurti* (this work is discussed elsewhere in this book).

Under the inspiring editorship of Mr. Dikshit, further books were published in the Krishnamurti Library series. These are evaluative studies of the teachings of K by different authors, such as Rene Fouere, Carlo Suares, Andre Niel, A.D. Dhopeshwarkar, A.J.G Methorst-Kuiper, Russell Balfour-Clarke and Susunaga Weeraperuma.

Students of the teachings should be particularly grateful to Mr. Dikshit. He will always be remembered as one of the outstanding pioneer torchbearers of the message of K throughout the world.

While K and I were admiring the great beauty of a snow-capped mountain in Switzerland, K discussed the bibliographies with me for the last time. He told me how glad he was that Chetana had published a second volume. "Please keep this work up-to-date," he requested. I remarked that the academic world can no longer overlook the teachings because, apart from their other advantages, "the bibliographies have proved that there now exists a distinct Krishnamurti literature." K nodded his head in agreement and said: "Only now I realize the full value of the bibliographies."

Sayings of J. Krishnamurti

It was Mr. Sudhakar S. Dikshit who commissioned me to compile an anthology of K quotations. I wholeheartedly accepted this proposal.

The part played by K in the origin of this book is best explained by quoting from its Preface:

"In May 1985 Sri J. Krishnamurti very kindly invited me for lunch at Arya Vihar, his home in Ojai,

California. This was a memorable occasion as it occurred only a few days after his 90th birthday. After a delicious vegetarian meal I informed Krishnaji that I was planning to compile for publication an anthology of quotations from his writings. He then inquired whether this book was going to be like *The Perennial Philosophy* by his friend, Aldous Huxley. I replied that it would be similar to Huxley's compilation in some respects but I would be selecting shorter passages and pithy sentences for inclusion. Then our discussion turned to the problem of finding a suitable title for the book. I suggested the title 'The Wisdom of Krishnamurti'. Krishnaji said: "That's too grand! Why not call it *Sayings of Krishnamurti?*" That he preferred a simple title to a grand one is so typical of his modest and self-effacing character.... Like a beautiful garland of many fragrant flowers, these selections have been taken from his utterances on a wide range of spiritual and philosophical subjects. I have painstakingly tried to present in this volume the quintessence of the message of one of the greatest teachers of all time."

K specifically requested me to implement Mr. Dikshit's proposal to prepare an anthology. But the Krishnamurti Foundation Trust refused to authorize its publication. Then I pointed an accusing finger at the Foundation for acting in defiance of K's clearly indicated wishes. Fortunately Mr. D. Rajagopal came to our rescue because at that time his K & R Foundation had the copyright for all K's books that belong to the pre-1968 period. Thanks to his goodness and respect for K's instructions, Mr. Rajagopal gladly granted the required permission.

It is necessary to reiterate that the title of this book was suggested by K himself a few months before he passed away. It is to him that this compilation is lovingly dedicated.

This work is the first one of its kind ever to be published relating to the teachings of K. It is a collection of 514 of his sayings up to the year 1968. Alphabetically arranged like a dictionary under 118 different subject headings, this invaluable reference book helps one to find out quickly what K has said on important subjects such as Awareness, Concentration, Fear, Happiness, Love, Meditation, etc. At the end of every quotation a statement is given indicating its source. In this way the interested reader is assisted not only to check the authenticity of a quotation but also its context.

After the book appeared in the shops, I was inundated with letters from readers who much appreciated it. The good reviews also testified to its usefulness and popularity: *The Vedanta Kesari (vol. 74 March 1987 p. 144):* "Weeraperuma has rendered a very valuable service to the general reader through this careful compilation and we hope he will follow it up with other choice selections of the ideas of one of the keenest intellects of the age."
The Times of India (December 14, 1986): "Susunaga Weeraperuma.... has strung together the most engaging insights from the Master's discourses. While the five hundred odd sayings not only enliven and arouse the mind of the reader, they also serve to emphasise the profundity of Krishnamurti's epigrammatic phrases. Employing the paradox, or by using the paradoxical statement, Krishnamurti has always made an impact on his listeners."

It is strange that even the Foundation praised the book. It appeared as if they had abandoned their hostile attitude to this publication. *Krishnamurti Foundation Bulletin* 52 Spring & Summer 1987 p.13: "This book is an extremely interesting anthology of quotations from Krishnamurti's talks and writings over a period of more than thirty years ... The extracts are meticulously chosen..."

When Mr. Dikshit sought permission to publish a companion volume of quotations, a second anthology for the post-1968 period, the Foundation turned him down once more. The letter from the Foundation states: "Mr. Weeraperuma's abilities and valuable work are much appreciated. However, the trustees are not able to give approval to anthologies because Krishnamurti did not consider them desirable and because to give approval for one now would encourage a proliferation of them in the future."

The statement that K did not consider anthologies desirable is grossly false. I have already explained that K clearly wanted me to compile an anthology. Besides, in the early 1950's K totally approved an anthology of his writings titled *The First and Last Freedom*. K particularly liked this book and his friend Aldous Huxley wrote the Preface to it. K also sanctioned the publication of another fine anthology titled *Meditations* (1979), consisting of 62 short passages and aphorisms gathered from previous works on the all-important subject of meditation and awareness.

The second reason given for the refusal of permission is equally ludicrous: "to give approval for one now would encourage a proliferation of them in the future." Why is the Foundation so opposed to a proliferation of books by K? Should not the teachings be made universally known by publishing more books?

The trustees of the Foundation brought themselves into considerable disrepute by obstructing Mr. Dikshit. Their decision was widely condemned and generally seen as one that is not going to promote but prevent the extensive diffusion of the teachings. Let posterity judge whether the Foundation or Mr. Dikshit was right in this matter.

Commentaries on the Teachings

There is a popular misconception that K was opposed to books by authors who discussed his teachings. I decided to obtain K's opinion of this issue by meeting him privately. With characteristic clarity K answered my question:

"Each person who has been touched by the teachings will want to spread them according to his talents. Some will become teachers or preachers. Others may like to express their understanding by writing books about the teachings."

"My problem", I explained, "is that I happen to be a conscientious writer. I am particularly careful not to misinterpret your teachings. Still, how can I be sure that I am not inadvertently distorting them?"

K said: "It is very simple. You must write in the light of your own understanding. Don't read into the teachings what is not intended. This means that you must be so intensely watchful of yourself so that you are no longer influenced by the various ideas, beliefs and experiences that have conditioned your outlook on life. When writing about the teachings, can you not state that you are only investigating them? Both you and your reader are going on a voyage of discovery together. Neither of you is sure what exactly K meant by a certain statement. Therefore you can never say "This is what K meant". All you can say is "*Probably* this is what K meant". It is good to use words like "perhaps" and "probably" because they introduce an element of doubt in the mind of the reader. Sir, if you do that you will not run the risk of becoming a misinterpreter."

I heeded the advice of K and cautionary measures were taken to prevent misinterpretation in the following three evaluative studies of K's teachings which were written by me:

Living and Dying from Moment to Moment: An investigation of J. Krishnamurti's Teaching. Bombay: Chetana, 1978 p.l:

"At the outset it is necessary to clarify certain matters. I do not stand here as Krishnamurti's spokesman: he has no spokesmen. For more than 50 years he has travelled throughout the world, lecturing on and discussing with varied audiences the most fundamental religious and philosophical issues. His expositions are very clear, precise, simple and free of jargon. Hence there is no need for spokesmen, intermediaries and interpreters. Anyone who is seriously interested can do no better than attend his talks or read his books, of which there are a great many. So, all I ask of you is to share with me the joy of investigating his teachings."

That Pathless Land : Essays on the beauty and uniqueness of J. Krishnamurti's teachings. Bombay: Chetana, 1983 p.l:

"That wondrous and sacred immensity, that vastness which is beyond the comprehension of the conditioned mind, has sometimes been alluded to as a 'movement' by Krishnamurti. 'This movement', he has remarked, 'can be described by thought but it is not of thought'. I must confess to never having experienced it. Then why do I write about matters which I have not understood? At least I can observe my attitudes to it; I can also watch attentively how the mind craves to speculate and theorise about it."

Bliss of Reality: Essays on J. Krishnamurti's extraordinary insights into life. Bombay: Chetana, 1984 p.v:

"This book is the outcome of a very careful examination of the teachings: it is not an interpretation of Krishnamurti's statements on life's deepest questions, but purely a searching *investigation* of them. I have looked at the teachings closely and critically, without interpreting them in the sense that I have not foisted into them any ideologies or beliefs."

His Last Visit to Sri Lanka

What follows is a slightly modified and enlarged version of a chapter from my book *That Pathless Land* (Bombay: Chetana, 1983).

Although K spent only a fortnight in Colombo, his visit will always remain an unforgettable experience for me. I had the opportunity of associating closely with him and feeling once again that K is unique amongst men. A nameless something animated his behaviour all the time which made him different from any other human being I have known. All his sayings and activities emanated from a certain centreless dimension that is altogether without parallel in ordinary persons.

K asked me whether there are people in Australia who are seriously interested in the teachings. I replied that in Australia, as elsewhere, such persons constituted a very small minority indeed. Later in our conversation he remarked that he was confining his activities to a very few places in the world and that it would not be possible for him to visit Australia.

K's fifth and last visit to Sri Lanka in November 1980 is historically important. He was a state guest and lived in a state mansion called Ackland House in Colombo. He was accorded all the honours and privileges that are usually reserved for visiting foreign dignitaries such as Presidents, Kings, Queens and Prime Ministers. I wonder whether any other country has ever treated him in this manner. Ministers of state called on him. The President and Prime Minister had interviews with him. The Prime Minister, Mr. R. Premadasa, after meeting K, remarked that "he is a marvellous soul". Mr. Premadasa, along with thousands of others, attended the public talks as well. As there was insufficient accommodation in the hall, all the discourses were broadcast over the national radio, which enabled millions to hear him. Friends in India, too, seized this opportunity to listen to this voice of sanity in the modern world.

K addressed the students of Jayawardhanapura University and was interviewed on TV by no less a person than the Minister for Information of Sri Lanka, Mr. Anandatissa de Alwis.

The Sri Lankan press was full of articles about the teachings in Sinhalese, Tamil and English. Some of the newspaper headlines are noteworthy: "To change society man has to change"; "Love, the only revolution"; "Nationalism, .religion have divided man"; "Krishnamurti — the perceptive philosopher".

Bhikkus (Buddhist monks) who live in hot climates

usually carry fans which are useful for fanning their perspiring bodies and faces. There is a certain kind of talipot palm fan that is associated with the Buddhist clergy. When I offered K such a fan he declined to accept it. He playfully said: "I'm not a Buddhist priest!"

Ascetic and shaven-headed Buddhist monks in their saffron-coloured robes mingled with the crowds to catch a glimpse of K. At a special meeting with Buddhist monks at his residence, K was asked an interesting question: Do you think at all? K replied that he thought only when it was necessary.

In matters that are mundane such as everything technological, thinking is obviously necessary. Thinking is necessary in the process of acquiring a skill or learning a language. But in the world of perception, is not thinking a hindrance and a factor making for distortion? Unless the mind is constantly stripped of its images, can it possibly see anew the various people we meet in our daily lives? A mind that is burdened with images can only experience suffering.

Buddhist monks were in rapport with K. They were invited by K to sit next to him on the dais. When they showed some reluctance to be near him, K laughingly said: "Don't be afraid. I won't bite!"

One of the sprightly young Buddhist monks declared that his mind is as liberated as that of K.

"If you are free," asked K doubtingly, "then why don't you discard your robes and dress like a layman?"

In reply to this suggestion, the monk said: "Mr. Krishnamurti, if you are really free yourself, what prevents you from wearing a yellow robe and also shaving your head?"

K: "Sir, freedom does not consist in conformity. A free man will not pattern himself upon any Teacher, idea nor belief."

Wherever he went K was received with affection and reverence. One suspects that not a few persons viewed K against the background of their image of the Buddha and interpreted the teachings in the light of Buddhist doctrine.

One of the things I discovered about K was that he held the Buddha in the highest esteem. The Buddha, in fact, was the *only* religious teacher he respected. When I raised certain philosophical issues, K made a surprising remark: "Why are you asking me these questions? Why don't you *probe deeply* into your own Buddhist literature? There you will find the answers."

At a press conference K was asked several probing questions and his answers to them were equally acute. Did he believe in reincarnation?

K: "What are you? A name conditioned by a culture and a religion, with ideals and a passport. Is that what is going to be reborn in the next life? To reincarnate there must be something permanent in you. If you are nothing but a series of reactions, what is there to reincarnate?"

On the evening of the 9th of November 1980, while he was addressing a particularly well-attended meeting in Colombo, K used a picturesque metaphor, in which self-observation was aptly described as the reading of "this book which is yourself". Within one is the whole story of mankind — its vast experiences, deep-rooted fears, anxieties, sorrows, pleasures and so forth. We are that book. It is an art to be able to read that book which is not printed by any publisher. Neither is this book for sale nor can it be bought in any bookshop. It is pointless resorting to an analyst for his book is the same as ours. The art of listening to what the book is saying is like observing a cloud, or palm leaves swaying in the wind. One cannot alter these things; one just observes them. Similarly, one listens to what the book is saying without attempting any kind of interpretation whatsoever. For one cannot tell the book what it should reveal. The art of listening also consists in never picking and choosing what one wishes to observe according to our particular likes and dislikes. If only we care to listen, without the pervasive influence of thought, then the book will reveal everything. It should not be overlooked that the reader of the book is not an entity separate from the book itself because "The book is you". This penetrating discourse, which dealt with many aspects of the teachings, was later published in the form of a booklet titled *The Book of Life.* Numerous copies of it were freely distributed in Calcutta on the occasion of K's visit to that city in November 1982.

The importance of constant watchfulness or awareness was repeatedly emphasized in every discussion and discourse. Without self-observation man was doomed to remain everlastingly in the bondage of his conditioned state. The urgency of delving deeply into the hidden recesses of the psyche was the theme of all his lectures: in a sense, that was the golden thread that interweaved all his utterances on various subjects. Listen very carefully to your thoughts. Watch yourself. See yourself exactly as you are without any distortion.

The great fondness for K's teachings in Sri Lanka was such that he was invited to give yet more talks there in November 1983. However, it was most unfortunate that a few months before K's planned arrival in Colombo, racial violence erupted in Sri Lanka. Many were killed and thousands were rendered homeless because of the activities of certain lawless elements. In a long letter to K, dated August 23rd 1983, I explained to him the nature of the large-scale disturbances. What follows are a few extracts from that letter:

My dear Krishnaji,

I think it would be very dangerous for you to visit Sri Lanka this coming November. Perhaps other friends have already indicated this fact. I am writing this letter because I am rather worried about your personal safety should you go ahead with the Colombo talks in a few months' time... I have written at length to point out that you run the risk of being physically attacked should you decide to go to Colombo. Although you are against racism and nationalism, these mad mobs will not see you as an apostle of peace. These crooked people will see you as a South Indian troublemaker. If I may suggest, it will be extremely dangerous for you to visit Sri Lanka right now. Therefore, I suggest that the talks be either cancelled or postponed. I hope that you are in the best of health.

Yours affectionately,
S. Weeraperuma

K sent me a message which was written by an associate of his who attended to his correspondence:

September 6, 1983

"Krishnaji has received your letter and appreciates very much your taking the trouble to write about his proposed visit to Sri Lanka. You will be glad to know that he had already written to say that he would be unable to go there. He was strongly advised against it by friends in India and your letter has confirmed what was already felt. He sends you his greetings and very good wishes..."

It was a great relief that K decided to stay away from the arena of a bloody commotion.

The Passing Away of Krishnamurti

The health of K was noticeably deteriorating during the last decade of his life. K's frail and delicate constitution was becoming weaker and the aged wrinkles and silvery hair increased his venerable appearance. His physical stature seemed to be shrinking. He was also losing weight and often he looked like a bag of bones. At times K resembled an emaciated yogi who had long been practising austerities on the banks of the Ganges. His thin long hands shook frequently with quick movements and the bags below the eyes bespoke tiredness. He felt fatigued after addressing public meetings or taking long walks. He needed longer periods of rest than ever before. Whenever I inquired after his health, K's usual reply was: "I'm all right I suppose." But was his health really all right?

It was obvious that K could no longer stand the strain and stress of exhausting schedules year in year out. Soon after K's eighty-fifth birthday, I wrote letters to one of his physicians and several trustees of the Krishnamurti Foundation. I requested them to take a certain course of action: Would it not be more beneficial to K's health, I argued, to persuade K to stay only in one place, preferably at his home in Ojai, instead of going on long wearisome intercontinental flights to give talks? Could not the video cassettes of his Ojai discourses be then distributed throughout the world?

The recipients of my letters turned a deaf ear to my suggestion. I was rudely told to mind my own business. It was also stated that K made his own decisions. I refused to believe that statement because K was often influenced by the views of the trustees in matters relating to his future programmes.

In 1980 K and I discussed the state of his health. I remarked that a long life span of 120 years was not beyond the reach of those yogis who looked after their bodies with great care. I presented K with a scientific book on the subject of longevity. K confidently said: "This body of mine may last another 12 years." Why then did K breathe his last breath in 1986 instead of 1992? I wish I knew the exact reasons that may have precipitated his expiry. K may have lived longer had he taken more rest because even during the last few years of his life he still had a very heavy workload.

During my sojourn in Bombay in January 1986 I heard the announcement that K was dying of cancer. The news from America that K's days were numbered caused me a great deal of distress. Actually the news did not come as a surprise because for nearly eighteen months prior to his death I had been having a premonition that the end of his life was fast approaching. Besides, Mr. S. Dikshit, who is a keen student of astrology, had forecasted that it was very unlikely that K would live beyond the month of February 1986 (how right his prediction turned out to be!). Mr. Dikshit, who had cast K's horoscope many years ago, advised me to accept philosophically the inevitability of death. Nothing is permanent and even the sun will get extinguished some day. Fortunately I had got permission to be away from my job in Australia for a period of six months, which enabled me to listen to K's last talks.

Sheila Ganatra, a longtime friend, wanted to present me with a return air ticket to America. She insisted that I should remain beside K during his final illness. Much though her idea appealed to me, I had to turn down her generous offer. I knew intuitively that in a situation of this kind K would naturally like to remain alone. And I was not wrong because several persons who were at Arya Vihar in Ojai informed me that K had been requesting certain visitors to go away. Apparently K wished to remain undisturbed on his deathbed.

On January 31, 1986 I addressed the Speakers' Forum in Bombay. The subject of my talk was "J. Krishnamurti's teachings for the explosion and transformation of the human mind". Please consider the following excerpts from that speech:

"On this occasion we are filled with sadness as our thoughts turn to Krishnaji's fatal illness. Krishnaji has been leading a pure and unblemished life. Why then has cancer struck him down? This is not the first time in history when it has been the lot of saintly individuals to experience physical suffering and die. Let us not forget that two other modern sages, Sri Ramakrishna Paramahamsa and Ramana Maharshi, were also the victims of painful cancer. Why is nature so unfair that some of her greatest and noblest sons have had to depart in this way ? It is surely important to ask such questions, although we may never succeed in finding the right answers to them. Probably there are certain incomprehensible mysteries, which will always remain beyond the reach of our finite minds."

"According to a certain school of thought Sri Ramakrishna Paramahamsa and Sri Ramana Maharshi died of cancer because they took on themselves the karma of some of their disciples. Such a theory is necessarily based on two questionable assumptions: first, that karma is transferable from one person to another; second, that it is possible to find Liberation vicariously: in other words, that man can be saved through the personal sacrifices of a saviour. Such theories, including the Christian belief that Jesus redeemed the world through his Crucifixion, are nothing more than wishful thinking."

"Krishnamurti is often described as an Indian sage. Well, he is Indian in the sense that he was born in India. There are certain aspects of Indian culture he much loves and admires, particularly Indian classical music and Indian art as well as the extraordinary beauty of the Sanskrit language. How he loves to chant slokas! But in another sense we do him an injustice to say that he is an Indian sage. Krishnamurti is not a sage whose inspiration comes from the age-old wisdom of the Vedas and the Upanishads or any other sacred scripture for that matter. It is necessary to understand that his realization of the Absolute is based solely on direct and personal experience. Naturally he questions the usefulness of sacred books and rejects all spiritual authorities and repeatedly refuses to be regarded as a guru. Now, both Sri Ramakrishna Paramahamsa and Ramana Maharshi were very well versed in the Hindu scriptures. But Krishnamurti is different from them because when he elucidates his teachings he hardly feels the need to quote from the scriptures at all."

"In the galaxy of enlightened teachers Krishnamurti is indeed a phenomenon. It is necessary to explain his uniqueness among religious philosophers. Mahavira spent twelve long years of preparatory self-purification, practising austerities and various sadhanas, before attaining the state of nirvana or absolute knowledge. Regarding the life of the Buddha, during the six years preceding the great spiritual metamorphosis of nirvana, which resulted in the dissolution of the self and hence the extinction of sorrow, he had to probe his mind thoroughly and meditate intensely. In recent times, Ramana Maharshi had to spend a considerable number of years as a solitary hermit in caves and temples in the course of his spiritual quest, which was characterized by such total absorption in the Self that he became indifferent to bodily discomforts and pains. It is really remarkable that Krishnamurti never had to practise sadhanas and austerities nor follow any of the traditional prescribed means to spiritual freedom. The available evidence suggests that the indescribable otherness held Krishnamurti very early in life. The exact date when he was blessed with the otherness remains unknown. However, I have no doubt that the otherness was already there, probably in a dormant state, when Bishop C.W. Leadbeater clairvoyantly noticed that the boy Krishnamurti had an aura which was devoid of selfishness. The extraordinariness of Krishnamurti consists in that early purity. As he grew older that otherness unfolded in the sense that its existence became clearer and more fully known. Here is a pure being, a lucky person, who did not have to confront the problem of purging his mind of impurities. Those of us who closely observed Krishnamurti were always conscious of his absolute purity. For instance, one day he was telling me about the cancer of hatred and divisiveness in society, which is largely caused by envy. Krishnamurti suddenly said: 'Never in my life have I been envious of another.' Neither did he harbour resentment against those who disliked his teachings."

On February 17, 1986 I received an overseas telegram stating that K had died in Ojai. That was the darkest day of my life. I felt as though a major part of myself had also died and disappeared; it was as if one's foundation had suddenly been removed. An irrational side of my grief-stricken mind kept on saying that K is still alive and keeping well in some unknown celestial realm. Such is the stubbornness of the mind that it refuses to resign itself to the finality of death. I still mourn the death of this devoted friend. My personal loss is nothing compared to the countless thousands in the world who will also miss him. The brightest star in the spiritual firmament is no more and one wonders whether the world will ever see the like of K again.

It was K who suggested that I should write down my thoughts and feelings whenever I was in the throes of an emotional crisis. "It helps to restore order within the mind," he assured me. What follows are a few jottings on the day of his death:

Liberated individuals may not find the dying process to be a terrible ordeal. Death is probably viewed by them as a welcome release from the 'last prison' — the body.

K did not want his death to be seen as an event of importance. Therefore he had requested that no fuss should be made over it. His instructions were that there should be no funeral service. In accordance with his wishes his mortal remains were cremated on the very day of his death.

It was my privilege to have closely associated with K from the days of my boyhood. During our numerous meetings over a period of three decades, not once did he tire of correcting me. He had infinite patience. It was sometimes not easy to be with K because he pulled you up for not being observant enough. The stimulus of his personal presence, alas, is no more. But if one is truly watchful of one's thoughts and feelings, really aware, then that alertness alone will be the awakening factor, the light, the flame that will burn away the dross of delusion. If one has that kind of eternal vigilance, then the passing away of K may not be as catastrophic as it seems.

The passing away of our beloved Krishnaji from our midst has been a matter of great sadness. For those of us who knew him well for many years it was a great blow. His physical presence is no more but his immortal message will be cherished forever.

When K passed away there were some who wept. We felt sad when he left us but did he feel sad to leave us? We were attached to him but was he attached to us? Was he attached to his reputation, his books or the Foundations which unworthily bear his name? He was not attached to *any* of these things, and in that sense he was a rare being with a mind that was totally unattached and pure.

Let us not build an organization or a temple around his name, for over the years one of the things he so vehemently denounced was organized religion, especially organized religion with vested interests. Now that the great sage is no longer with us, what needs to be done to keep alive the flame of his message?

I think that any person who is seriously interested in what K said can do no better than read and read again his many books. Fortunately there are also in existence many audio cassettes and video cassettes of his talks and interviews, which will enable posterity to know K as though he were still alive.

Scepticism was once described by K as a precious ointment: it burns but it also heals. K wanted us to question everything, including his own statements. If we question everything and destroy every psychological barrier then perhaps the miracle of transformation may take place.

Appendices

Dialogues between Krishnamurti and the Author

Appreciation of Devotional Music

SW: *Krishnaji, I much enjoyed the concert last night. I have come to India to listen to such melodious music. It was such a treat.*

K : Yes. It was a marvellous performance.

SW: *What puzzles me is why you participated in the chanting of Bhajans. I was observing you very closely. You were in the front row and chanting Vedic hymns! I am not against Vedic hymns for I love them very much myself. But please may I ask why you have often expressed strong disapproval of any kind of worship? You condemn worship but yesterday you were joining others in worship!*

K : One can listen to an enchanting Bhajan and still not be influenced by its ideas. It is possible to listen to a Sloka or Bhajan and experience the magical effects of the sounds on the mind and totally ignore all the myths, legends, beliefs and concepts that are so much part of the Indian classical tradition. Have you tried enjoying a Meera Bhajan without believing in Krishna or any deity?

SW: *I think a Bhajan becomes more meaningful when one is aware that it is addressed to a particular deity. A Bhajan is a devotional outpouring of the heart.*

K : Oh, no! I wouldn't call that devotion. Real devotion is motiveless. It is a state of not asking anything. But when you stand before an altar and offer Puja and then ask favours in return, that is psychological bribery, isn't that so? You try to bargain with the deity. You are telling the deity: "I am offering you this and you must provide me with that in return." But real devotion is a state in which the mind is not focussed on any particular object, person, deity, belief or idea.

SW: *Are you saying that a true devotee has an objectless state of mind?*

K : Exactly. As I was saying, the right way to listen to any hymn or devotional chant is to experience only the sound — its movements of melancholic supplication and joyous ecstasy, and just remain there, not allowing your mind to get conditioned by the particular religious ideas and beliefs that nearly always go hand in hand with the music. Then you will find that all kinds of devotional music are fundamentally the same.

SW: *Shall I organize a concert of Western classical music for you?*

K : Don't trouble yourself. I will have many opportunities of listening to Western classical music when I go to Europe.

SW: *I'm fond of Bach, Beethoven and Handel.*

K : I also like those composers. Do you follow what I am saying? If you listen carefully you will find that every kind of devotional music, regardless of where in the world it originated in, has certain common elements. What are these elements? Haven't you noticed that all devotional music is a kind of asking, crying, begging?

SW: *That quality makes the music very touching. I understand what you are saying.*

K : I wonder whether you have ever listened to a child crying. Have you?

SW: *The noise of children screaming and crying gets on my nerves! I want to run away!*

K : If you have really listened to a child crying with all your heart and mind, as I have done, not listening partially but listening fully with undivided attention, then you will also feel like crying. You will want to hold the hand of the child and join him or her in the crying. Unless you have a pure heart you will not be capable of doing that. I am describing the state of true devotion — not the nonsensical devotion of a stupid mind that offers flowers and incense to an image made by the hand or the mind.

SW: *Would you call that pure bhakti?*

K : The name is not important. You may give it any name you like but do you have that quality of feeling?

SW: *I often go to concerts but the difficulty is that after listening to the first few bars of a song my mind starts wandering.*

K : Then wander with your mind and find out why your attention is shifting from one thing to another.

SW: *What you are suggesting sounds excellent but I have tried it out in practice and often I am unsuccessful.*

K : Keep on trying and never give up.

SW: *Somewhere in your writings you have stated that music is to be found not in the notes but in the interval between the notes. I have failed to grasp the full significance of your statement.*

K : Notes in themselves are quite meaningless, aren't they? Similarly, when you read a book, the words in themselves have no meaning at all. Notes and words are meaningless sounds. It is in the interval between words, in the state of silence between words, that you capture the meaning of what the writer is trying to convey. So don't get lost in the technical side of music. To appreciate a piece of music it is not absolutely essential to have the ability to read it. Understanding comes only when the mind is silent. And don't regard music as an escape or as a drug that may induce silence. That silence comes naturally, effortlessly, when you understand. Music is born in that silence. That silence is the source of all creation. That primordial silence has no beginning and no end. That silence, the eternal, is beyond the reach of the intellect.

Remain Anonymous All Your Life

SW: *Krishnaji, I have just read an interesting item of news in today's evening paper. A certain member of the Colombo Municipal Council will be introducing a motion concerning you at the next meeting of the Council. His motion states that you should be accorded a civic reception by the Municipal Council of the city of Colombo.*

K : What exactly takes place at a civic reception?

SW: *Civic receptions are accorded only to distinguished individuals by the mayor and prominent citizens.*

K : Good Lord! I am a poor Mr. Nobody whose individuality has been extinguished! Not distinguished but extinguished! (loud laughter).

SW: *At the reception probably the Prime Minister will welcome you and speeches will be made in honour of you. You will be presented with a scroll signed by eminent persons from Sri Lanka.*

K : What will the scroll contain?

SW: *Surely they will refer to your various achievements and your spirituality.*

K : I don't want a certificate from anybody!

SW: *Krishnaji, I think it will be a great pity if you turn down such an invitation. What an opportunity to make a fine speech! At least a few of the politicians who listen to you may become permanently interested in your teachings. Why should you deprive them of the benefit of your message?*

K : If those politicians are seriously interested in what I have to say, what prevents them from attending my public talks? Sir, you are so naive that you fail to see through the behaviour of politicians. Can't you see that they are all politically motivated? I refuse to be used by politicians. I avoid them.

SW: *You say that you avoid politicians but you associate with Mrs. Indira Gandhi!*

K : That's different! Indira is an old friend. Her father Pundit Nehru used to visit Amma (Dr. Annie Besant) and me when we were in Benares.

SW: *Please reconsider what I have suggested.*

K : I am sorry. Please telephone this member of

the Municipal Council and ask him to withdraw his motion from the agenda. Will you please telephone him immediately?

SW: *Yes, I will. But if they insist on having a ceremony in honour of you, I don't think you can stop them from doing it.*

K : Let them do what they like but I will not be there!

SW: *I will be telephoning soon.*

K : Whatever you may do in life or wherever you may happen to live, always avoid publicity. Do not crave to be in the limelight. The other day I was telling some people that the desire to see your photograph published in the newspapers is the greatest vulgarity. Shun the vulgar crowds and lead a righteous life that is unbeknown to your friends, relatives and associates. Like a mighty tree that is hidden deep in the forest, remain anonymous all your life.

SW: *Why are you against politicians? Surely some of them are genuinely desirous of helping society.*

K : Anyone who is driven by ambition and the lust for power simply cannot be good. They are responsible for so much mischief in the world. In India people make a great fuss over their leading politicians. Thousands stand in the burning sun for hours just to see an important politician as though he were some kind of strange animal! Why give them such importance when you know that they aspire after political leadership only because they want to feather their own nests? Politicians reek of corruption. So a good person has to keep away from politicians and all their activities. If you wish to help the poor and improve social conditions, then the first step is to be a good person yourself. That very goodness will have a beneficial impact on society.

Peace in a Strife-torn Country

K : I wonder why they call this island a Buddhist country. Can a territory have a religion or a race?

SW: *One has to realize that the vast majority of inhabitants of Sri Lanka are Buddhists. They may not strictly adhere to the Buddha's teachings but they regard themselves as Buddhists.*

K : You mean they are Buddhists in name only?

SW: *That is unfortunately so.*

K : What was there before the introduction of Buddhism?

SW: *I do not know the answer to that question. According to certain historians, there prevailed here a kind of animism. It was believed that all objects, even inanimate objects, were endowed with souls. So the people worshipped the spirits that were supposed to dwell in trees and animals and lots of other objects.*

K : Man has always been a worshipper. The desire to worship can be traced back to man's savage past and extends right up to the present day when he is still a worshipper. Man worships today a highly refined concept of God; it is a very sophisticated belief. This shows that the mind of man has always been, and still remains, haunted by fear and anxiety. It is very simple.

The urge to worship arises only because of the existence of fear. If you can remove fear from his psyche, man will immediately cease being a worshipper.

SW: *I think it is generally agreed that Buddhism was introduced to Sri Lanka in the year 246 B.C. The great Buddhist Emperor Asoka persuaded his own son, the monk Mahinda, to visit Sri Lanka and convert this land to Buddhism. According to tradition, this country was thrice visited by the Buddha himself.*

K : You mean to say that he travelled here all the way from Benares some 2,500 years ago? Do you believe that?

SW: *He is supposed to have travelled here by levitation.*

K : You mean to say that he rose and floated in the air? Ah, I know. The Buddha must have taken an Air India flight to Colombo! (laughter).

SW: *I know that your remark was meant jokingly. But every year thousands of Buddhist pilgrims go to those places in Sri Lanka which are believed to have been touched by the feet of the Buddha. Rightly or wrongly the Buddhists of Sri Lanka feel that they are the rightful custodians of the Buddha's doctrines. When Buddhism virtually died out in the land of its birth, thanks to Hindu orthodoxy, these teachings were protected in Sri Lanka. Throughout the centuries various Sinhalese kings took measures to ensure the survival of Buddhism. That is why the Sinhalese proudly regard themselves as the defenders of Buddhism.*

K : So the people of this country are the self-appointed custodians of Buddhism! Sir, don't you see the absurdity of what you are saying?

SW: *I do not personally believe in this theory that the Sinhalese are destined to be the protectors of Buddhism. I am merely reporting to you the existence of this belief.*

K : If what the Buddha preached was the Truth, then that Truth can look after itself. That Truth does not belong to any person or nation. That Truth is neither yours nor mine. Truth is always there, regardless of whether a Buddha arises in the world to give utterance to it. That Truth, which is timeless and indestructible, cannot be stolen nor destroyed.

SW: *How true! I have conveyed all these facts to you because it is necessary to understand the myths that sustain Sinhalese nationalism.*

K : Why, Sir, the Sinhalese are not the only people who have various beliefs to fortify their identity.

SW: *The Jews, for instance, are wedded to the idea that they are the chosen people. And the Bible supports their racism.*

K : The Bible can be quoted to prove all kinds of contradictory beliefs and ideas. So let us leave aside the Bible and all these other so-called sacred literature. When you are very clear in your mind you will not want to rely on any sacred text.

SW: *Fortunately, all the teachings attributed to the Buddha have been recorded for the benefit of posterity. His discourses have been written down in Pali, Sanskrit and other languages.*

K : No language, however ancient or noble, can record the Truth. The Truth, which is living and moving from moment to moment, cannot be reduced to writing. My friend Aldous Huxley was fond of quoting a wise saying that the Buddha never preached the Truth because the Buddha was only too well aware of the fact that Truth is inexpressible. Truth is something that has to be experienced personally from moment to moment. It is a dynamic movement, understand? Only something that is dead can be recorded in books.

SW: *It is all very well for you to criticize books, but without them could I ever have known about the Buddha's life and his lofty ideas?*

K : The Buddha never taught any ideas. Enlightened beings are not concerned with ideas. Ideas are the toys of intellectuals and priests. Ideas condition your mind. The person who is really serious will regard ideas as useless things. A mind that is teeming with ideas has no space within it and hence incapable of clarity, intelligence, light.

SW: *Please excuse me for having used the wrong phrase. I should have said 'lofty insights' of the Buddha instead of 'lofty ideas'.*

K : Do you think that the Buddha's insights have made this country any different from the rest of the world? Are the people of Sri Lanka highly intelligent? Are they aware of the great beauty of this land? This country is extraordinarily beautiful. Do the people observe the marvellous wind-driven white clouds, the silhouette of the tall coconut palms against the deep blue sky or the colourful birds and flowers? Have you looked out of the window and noticed that gigantic tamarind tree?

SW: *I do not believe that the people of Sri Lanka are fundamentally different from the rest of humanity. You will be shocked to know that the crime rate here is pretty high. The vast majority of Buddhists unashamedly eat meat and fish.*

K : And they call themselves Buddhists!

SW: *This country is also cursed with racial conflict between the Sinhalese and the Tamils. The Tamils, who are a minority of eighteen percent of the population, want to establish their own separate state because they complain that they are discriminated against by the majority Sinhalese. During the last few years thousands of persons have lost their lives because of racial violence.*

K : What is the root of violence?

SW: *So far as Sri Lanka is concerned, I think the violence is caused by mutual fear. The minority Tamils fear the majority Sinhalese and the Sinhalese also fear the Tamils because over the centuries Sri Lanka was frequently invaded by Tamilian princes and armies. Krishnaji, what is your solution to this problem?*

K : The Sinhalese and the Tamils have lived together in this lovely island for nearly two thousand years. Now, why did one group of people fail to merge into the other? Both groups are responsible for failing to combine into an integrated whole. When a Sinhalese person identifies himself with the Sinhalese race, he feels, does he not, that he is somehow different from his Tamilian neighbour? So is it possible to drop the labels 'Sinhalese' and 'Tamil'? Why do we give ourselves stupid labels? These labels generate hatred. Sir, what are you? You are only a bundle of thoughts, memories, desires, fears, hurts and a thousand conditioning influences. Why give this bundle a label? Why give it a name? And is the bundle that you carry with you in your mind any different from the bundle carried by someone who is supposed to belong to another race? Are you any different from the rest of mankind? Every human being is caught up in a common psychological stream. If you can somehow make the people realize this obvious truth then perhaps there will be peace in this strife-torn country.

SW: *Don't you also think that violence is caused because our hearts are devoid of compassion?*

K : That is true but compassion cannot be cultivated. Compassion cannot be practised. You cannot practise brotherhood. That is why all the religions of the world have failed to change the nature of man. The quality of compassion comes suddenly, unexpectedly, when you have cleared up the psychological mess within yourself.

SW: *Compassion is a very important aspect of the Buddha's teachings.*

K : That may be so but do not confine compassion to Buddhism or any other teaching. Sir, as I see it, a true Buddhist is someone who is always kind, generous, loving, forgiving and considerate towards all living beings. A true Buddhist would not want to hurt any living creature. Now, is it not possible to have all these virtues without calling yourself a Buddhist? For the moment you identify yourself with any group or sect you inevitably create conflict and division, don't you?

SW: *Why do I want to identify myself with something else?*

K : In yourself you are nothing. If you strip yourself of all your thoughts, what is left? You are absolutely nothing. As you find this nothingness so frightening, you like to cover it up by wanting to identify yourself with a guru, religion, sect, race or country. From the very earliest times man has been tribal in his outlook because he wanted to identify himself with a group or a cause. He sought to strengthen his non-existent sense of 'I' through a process of identification.

Only Peace Within will Ensure Peace Without

SW: *Decades ago you said "The world problem is the individual problem and the individual problem is the world problem." Nowadays one of your favourite sayings is "You are the world and the world is you." There is no fundamental difference between these two sayings of yours. Do you still maintain that social welfare work will not create a better society?*

K : I am not opposed to improving the living standards of people. We obviously need better houses, improved sanitation, a cleaner environment and right nutrition. Any decent government must provide these essentials.

SW: *Therefore I take it that you are not opposed to material progress.*

K : Why should I be opposed to technological advancement? We are in the age of the jet aircraft and who wants to go back to the days of the bullock cart?

SW: *Our rate of material progress is so fast that before long poverty may completely disappear. We will live longer. As we increase our material prosperity, do you think that man will gradually shed his anti-social traits? Every person will have all the basic necessities of life with the result that he may not feel the need to steal from those who are well-off. Rich countries may not want to conquer and colonize poor ones. There will be fewer wars.*

K : You are a dreamer!

SW: *Is it not a fact that you lead a more comfortable life than your grandparents ever did? Unlike yourself, your ancestors were not globetrotters.*

K : I do not particularly enjoy travelling in aeroplanes. I tolerate it only because it is the fastest means of travel between countries.

SW: *Can you deny the fact that we have improved tremendously?*

K : It depends on what you mean by that word "improve". Material goods we certainly have in abundance but psychologically we have stagnated.

SW: *Would you please care to elaborate on that statement?*

K : Primitive man pelted his enemies with rocks and stones. Thousands of years later, modern man fights his enemies with guns and grenades and what have you. Primitive man was violent and aggressive and so are we. Do you call that progress?

SW: *What you are complaining about is a favourite theme of moralists and theologians who keep on telling us that we are still in our spiritual childhood.*

K : Not childhood but infancy!

SW: *Let me examine the statement that "You are the world and the world is you". Are you implying that I am personally responsible for the fighting that is going on in the Middle East between the Jews and the Arabs? I have done nothing to cause or even aggravate the looting, shooting and fighting which are daily occurrences in those parts of the world. In that sense it does not seem right to state that "I am the world and the world is me".*

K : May I ask you a personal question?

SW: *Yes. You are free to ask me any question.*

K : Have you cleansed your mind and heart of violence?

SW: *I do not regard myself as being a violent person. But I do lose my temper sometimes in trying situations.*

K : Anger is a form of violence. Do you agree?

SW: *It is a mild form of violence.*

K : It is mild at the beginning but it leads to acts of violence later.

SW: *Perhaps I am slightly violent.*

K : That is a ridiculous thing to say! You are either violent or your mind is devoid of violence. The distinction is very clear-cut. You cannot be both violent and devoid of violence at the same time. Please listen carefully to what I am saying. Either you are an honest man or a dishonest man. You can never say "I am slightly dishonest"! If you are "slightly dishonest" it only means that you have a dishonest mind. Sir, it is like the curate's egg: if the egg is fresh it can be eaten but if it is even slightly rotten then you have to discard it. Sir, do you have the honesty to admit that you are a violent person?

SW: *Yes, I am violent. So what?*

K : Do you realize that your violence is qualitatively not different from the violence that is raging through the Middle East?

SW: *Yes, qualitatively it is the same violence but not quantitatively.*

K : The degree of violence is unimportant. The extent of violence does not alter the fact that you are already suffering from the fever of violence. Sir, an invisible microscopic virus can cause a vast epidemic that kills millions. Similarly, the tiniest bit of violence within you could precipitate a world war.

SW: *Krishnaji, you make me feel very guilty.*

K : You have got to probe into the depths of your mind and uproot all your ill will. Unless you are prepared to do that what right have you to talk about bringing peace to the Middle East?

SW: *I will of course make a special effort to get rid of violence and change myself.*

K : Wait a minute! Is not the maker of effort that tries to eliminate violence, a form of violence itself? When violence attempts to subjugate violence there will be more violence. Do you see the complexity of the problem?

SW: *All I have to do is recognise the existence of violence. If the fact of violence is fully acknowledged and seen, then that very act of seeing will result in the dissolution of violence.*

K : Quite right. The very act of seeing is the doing. When you observe the existence of violence that very observation is itself the factor which brings about the miracle of change.

SW: *The number of sovereign states in the world is rapidly increasing.*

K : Consequently there are more armies, more navies, more airforces and more generals. Any crazy President or Prime Minister can set the world on fire.

SW: *What are your views on the campaigns for banning nuclear weapons?*

K : Why don't they campaign against the banning of *all* weapons? It is not enough to get excited about the dangers of radiation. What is necessary is the elimination of *all* forms of violence.

SW: *Is it not the responsibility of every government to keep the peace within its national frontiers?*

K : One should distrust the state. The state originates in violence and is maintained by resorting to violence. Every state is founded on violence because it has to support an army and a police to make sure that its laws and decisions are obeyed. Every state is also expected to defend itself when attacked by invaders and aggressors. Do not overlook the fact that the state is an instrument of violence. This is not a theory but a historical fact. So why expect the state to banish violence when it is itself an instrument of violence? Do you understand the problem? Can you ever clean a dirty floor by using dirty water? So do not pin your hopes on the state, if you seriously want peace because, as I explained, the state is the very enemy of peace for it financially supports the institution of war.

SW: *We seem to be coming back to your main thesis that there will be no peace in the world unless man is himself peaceful first as a consequence of a deep inner spiritual transformation. Such a view necessarily implies that it is foolish to depend on governments or the United Nations to establish peace.*

K : What you are, your government is. Governments can only reflect what you actually are.

SW: *Therefore the most important question is why violence is so much part of our nature.*

K : So long as man is enslaved to his self, the ego, the sense of 'I', he will want to assert himself. And all assertions of the ego are forms of violence. Have you observed the various ways by which the ego expresses itself? '*My* country', '*my* caste','*my* family', '*my* beliefs', '*my* reputation' — these are different kinds of self-assertion. If you derive a great sense of self-fulfilment and satisfaction from a certain activity, then are you not using that activity to assert your ego? And as I just said, whoever asserts himself is responsible for violence in the world. The do-gooders who engage themselves in various social welfare activities, the politicians, the philanthropists, are all subtly asserting their egos. The ego is not concerned with the welfare of society; it is only interested in its own survival and lust for power. Therefore the ego is given to ruthlessness and violence.

SW: *There will be peace on earth only if we care to wipe away our egos.*

K : The ego can never wipe itself away because it is everlastingly struggling to assert itself either consciously or unconsciously.

SW: *There will be peace on earth only if our egos drop away.*

K : Exactly.

SW: *Finally, I wish to ask this question. What is the best form of government?*

K : Once again you are moving away from the essential issue. From time immemorial philosophers have been producing blueprints for a new world. The ancient Greeks believed that their city state was the ideal form of government. Today the capitalists and the communists also maintain that their particular systems of government are the best. As long as man remains animalistic there will never be a perfect system. But if we succeed in changing the psyche of man, then he will surely bring his society to a state of perfection.

Action Without Thought

SW : *In one of your talks you strongly disapproved of competitive sports. If I have understood you correctly, you were saying that the great need of the modern world is not the spirit of competition but that of cooperation.*

K : It is fairly obvious that competition is causing the fragmentation of the world. We see how the world is broken up economically, socially and politically. This planet has been divided into nation states. And when countries compete with one another there will inevitably be tension, suspicion, unfriendliness, misunderstanding and eventually war.

SW: *You condemn every manifestation of the competitive spirit, be it in the playing fields or the examination halls of schools and universities, and yet you privately enjoy competitive sports. For instance, this afternoon I saw you with a group of students in the television lounge. All of you were glued to the television set for several hours. With relish you were watching Cassius Clay Mohammed Ali, the American heavyweight boxer, defending his world title. When one of the poor boxers was rudely knocked unconscious and was therefore unable to rise, the students loudly applauded. And you of all persons, dressed in your blue jeans, shouted 'bravo, bravo!' It was a sight that shocked me.*

K : All these past years you were having a certain impression of me and now you find that your impression does not correspond with reality. You believed that K always dresses and acts in a certain way and now you are disappointed. Why do you have an image of K? Can't you see that when you form an image you soon become its prisoner? Drop the image! I don't have any image of myself. Have you ever tried to denude the mind of all its accumulated images?

SW: *It is all very well for you to philosophize but have you no sympathy for the poor fellow who fell down unconscious? Krishnaji, I am sure that you are acquainted with the medical facts relating to boxing and wrestling. There is a campaign in England to ban these sports because the risk of brain damage to participants is high.*

K : What action is being taken to prevent the psychological damage caused by having images? Sir, please don't stand there. Sit on the settee and let us talk over together the little things that worry you. Shall we begin with the blue jeans? (laughter). I have been given several pairs of jeans. They are excellent trousers for walking in the woods. Would you like to have a pair?

SW: *It is very kind of you, Krishnaji, but my trouser size is different from yours. I have to decline your generous offer.*

K : The other day an Indian gentleman who attended one of my talks angrily asked me why I don't wear kurtas and pyjamas in England.

SW: *And what was your answer?*

K : I'm sure he already knew the reason for not wearing Indian clothes in England. This is a cold country. One must dress according to the climate. Besides, Indian clothes would attract a lot of attention here. Right living is a great art. One should live in such a way that no one notices your presence. Live righteously but never display your righteousness.

SW: *Shall we discuss boxing?*

K : I am opposed to all blood sports such as foxhunting. Once on television I saw a poor helpless deer being tortured by hunters and I turned away in revulsion. I switched the television off. Anyone who is sensitive will surely respond in that way. Man is a savage at heart and he enjoys all kinds of cruelties that are perpetrated in the name of sport.

SW: *I suppose we vicariously enjoy seeing sadistic activities. We are scared of the consequences of behaving in a wicked way ourselves, so we like to see the wicked deeds of others.*

K: Not only that but there is also this insatiable need for continuous excitement. We cannot live with ourselves and face the emptiness within. Therefore this so-called civilization of ours provides all manner of escapes through sports, drugs, sex and religion.

SW: *I have noticed how wildly cheering football crowds give vent to their pent-up emotions, frustrations, aggression and so forth.*

K : In my youth I was a fairly good tennis player. I have seen how professional players take great pride in what they can do. There is much pleasure in showing off what you alone can do and what others cannot do. Unless a boxing champion is strongly motivated and has a very big ego he would not be able to go through the ordeal of all those long hours of discipline and training. Human beings are willing to suffer hardships in order to achieve something. The sense of 'me' is always seeking expansion, whether in the field of sport or in the so-called spiritual world. How the yogis practise austerities to acquire psychic powers! Once they have got some power or learned to perform a silly trick, how they love to make a parade of it!

SW: *I understand nearly everything you have explained. May I very respectfully ask you a personal question?*

K : You may.

SW: *Do you get some kind of a kick out of watching boxing?*

K : A boxer or a wrestler, if he wants to win, must act spontaneously. He can never know in advance the direction from which he is going to be attacked in a match. He must act quickly. There is no time to think carefully and then act. So he has to put aside the machinery of his mind and act without thought. When your behaviour is governed by the dictates of thought then you are merely *reacting* to the challenges of life. And your life is nothing but a series of such reactions. But there is quite a different way of meeting the challenges of life. There is a great joy when you cease reacting according to thought but start *responding* to life without it.

The Nature of Memory

SW: *I find that I am becoming rather forgetful as I grow older. I do not know whether forgetfulness is related to age.*

K : Forgetfulness is not related to age. Children can be just as forgetful as adults. Are you vitally interested in this problem?

SW: *I am particularly interested in it. I belong to an academic profession. As a librarian I have to remember masses of facts and figures. I have recently noticed that I am no longer a quick efficient worker because I am handicapped by a poor memory.*

K : First of all I think we should distinguish between two types of memory. There is 'factual memory' and 'psychological memory'.

SW: *I take it that 'factual memory' is information or technical data. It is knowledge of a factual kind.*

K : Yes. 'Factual memory' consists of information of all sorts. At school you must have learned history and geography. Now all that is 'factual memory'. 'Factual memory' is obviously important. We need it for survival. If I don't remember what your face looks like, I will not be able to recognize you the next time we meet. An engineer has to know a great deal before he is able to build a bridge or construct a house. Knowledge keeps on increasing at a very fast rate, especially technical knowledge.

SW: *It is snowballing.*

K : The engineers of the future will have to study much more than today's engineers. The mind has a great capacity to accumulate information. It has extraordinary faculties but we are not using all our faculties.

SW: *Are you suggesting that there is a wasteful under-utilization of our brains?*

K : You may put it that way if you like. There is a certain sluggishness and we do not fully use our brains.

SW: *You have described 'factual memory' very well. I have never had difficulty understanding it. But I have a vague notion of 'psychological memory'. By the phrase 'psychological memory' do you mean non-factual memory?*

K : 'Psychological memory' is not non-factual. It is very factual.

SW: *I suppose you mean that 'psychological memory' is undesirable whereas 'factual memory' is desirable?*

K: Let us be clear about what is 'psychological memory'. I remember what your face looks like. We have already called that 'factual memory'. Now, if I were to like the look of your face or hate it, that like or dislike will naturally influence my attitude to you. Our likes and dislikes constitute 'psychological memory'. Do you understand? Sir, all your fears, hates, anxieties, hopes, hurts, ambitions — all that is 'psychological memory'.

SW: *I understand the two types of memory. They are very closely interrelated. I don't know where exactly one kind of memory ends and the other begins. In the example you have considered, the impression of my face that is registered in your mind is called 'factual memory'. Your disliking the face is called 'psychological memory'. But isn't your disliking it also a fact?*

K : Of course it is a fact. It is not something imagined. But the moment I allow that dislike to influence my attitude to you, then I am under the control of 'psychological memory'. So is it possible to have a mind that is all the time operating at the level of 'factual memory' and not at the level of 'psychological memory'? It is 'psychological memory' that conditions the mind and distorts perception.

SW: *Shall we examine this question again? I think I must be very clear about it. My face happens to be very ugly. That ugliness is a fact.*

K : I remember a face exactly as it is, without calling it either 'ugly' or 'beautiful'.

SW: *But the ugliness is a fact.*

K : It is the way I react to your face that constitutes 'psychological memory'.

SW: *Aren't you repelled by ugliness and attracted by beauty?*

K : You should watch your reactions as they arise. When you see a reaction completely, it gets burnt away in a jiffy.

SW: *In that way the mind would be kept uncontaminated all the time.*

K : That is right. I have said that the reaction gets erased when the mind is passively alert. Have you also observed that the mind will not react at all when it does not name its reactions? When the face is called 'ugly' or 'handsome', are you not distorting your perception by introducing the past? You resuscitate the past the moment you verbalize. Words are the past. So if I avoid calling the face 'ugly' or 'beautiful', I avoid past associations, which means that it becomes possible to see the face exactly as it is, and hence I develop neither feelings of attraction nor revulsion. The mind then remains free.

SW: *We have discussed something that is extremely important, although the conversation has* *drifted from the subject of forgetfulness to another subject.*

K : You were saying that you are forgetful.

SW: *Yes. The ability to retain factual data in my mind seems to be declining.*

K : What have you been doing about it?

SW: *Well, every night before falling asleep I recall the details of what I experienced during the day. It is a yogic mental exercise. I read that the retentive capacity of the brain can be strengthened by doing this exercise. The theory is that the muscles of memory, so to speak, get stronger when they are frequently flexed. What the mind has learned should be constantly recalled and thereby kept afresh. How easily one forgets a foreign language when it has not been used for a considerable time! In Buddhist temples I have seen monks not only laboriously memorising the scriptures but also regularly reciting them as a means of not forgetting them.*

K : I knew a Sannyasin who learned the entire *Bhagavad Gita* by heart. He could even recite the book backwards and of course then it was quite meaningless. People surrounded him and admired his mental gymnastics! You might as well train a parrot to give such performances.

SW: *A good memory is a very useful asset in life.*

K : Did your memory improve after doing that exercise?

SW: *By recalling the day's events I found that my mind became more orderly but there was no significant improvement in the mind's retentive capacity.*

K : I have met persons with photographic minds. With extraordinary exactness they could remember almost anything. But I have found that such persons are not quick at noticing what is happening within themselves as well as outside themselves. They are not very observant.

SW: *It will be excellent to have an observant mind which is also photographic at the same time.*

K : I've never met a person with such a mind.

SW: *Every morning for five minutes I practise sirshasana (standing on the head) because I learned from Swami Sivananda of Rishikesh that this asana is particularly good for the brain. According to him 'memory improves admirably'.*

K : I also do this asana but not with the intention of having a good memory. This asana is good for the nerves.

SW: *Then it must also be good for the brain.*

K : Do you sleep soundly?

SW: *There are days when I do not sleep well.*

K : When the brain has not properly rested the body becomes tense and irritable. But when the whole system is relaxed memories will surface easily. Are you taking the right food? I have been told that a protein deficiency could impair the efficient functioning of the brain. You must investigate this possibility because I know that persons of Asian origin often suffer from a lack of protein. Shall I test your memory?

SW: *You may do so.*

K : Sir, how did you spend last Saturday evening?

SW: *I don't remember the details. Perhaps I went*

for a walk but I have no recollection of where I walked.

K : What is the name of the latest best-seller?

SW: *There are several best-sellers.*

K : What are their names?

SW: *I forget.*

K : Do you remember the name of your best friend?

SW: *Of course I do.*

K : Sir, it is so simple. The mind remembers what is pleasant and represses those memories that are unpleasant. Don't you like to forget disturbing insults and criticisms? And aren't you attached to all the complimentary remarks of others about your work? If you really enjoyed your work would you be having this problem? Tell me, are you happily employed?

SW: *At one time I much enjoyed my job but nowadays I loathe having to do such an enormous amount of work in my office.*

K : Your antipathy towards your work and your employer is obviously obstructing the surfacing of memories associated with your work. Any kind of agitation, disturbance or worry prevents the unconscious from communicating with the conscious. Are you fully aware of the existence of this antipathy? Dig it out and examine it. After a few weeks of doing this you can let me know whether your memory has improved.

SW: *Krishnaji, your friends know only too well that you have a bad memory.*

K : That is true. If I haven't seen someone for about ten years I forget that person completely. Some persons have been very offended because I failed to recognize them. It cannot be helped. That is the way I am.

SW: *Have you taken any remedial measures to improve your memory?*

K : I don't want to improve myself. I am not interested in achieving anything. Knowing the state of *what is*, the living now, is immensely more important than bothering your head about *what should be*.

SW: *I am puzzled by the fact that all this time you were suggesting ways of improving my memory but now I find that you are not interested in improving your own memory.*

K : In ancient times certain philosophers and educationists regarded the mind as a receptacle for knowledge. The mind was seen as a useful storehouse of knowledge. In the modern world we have computers that are capable of storing information not only faster than the human mind but also far more accurately. Why burden your mind with knowledge when there are computers to do that work? What then is the purpose of the mind? Surely the mind should be used as an instrument of observation without distortion. Seeing rightly, intelligent observation, observation without the observer, is the role of the mind. The world is such a lovely place, full of colour and light and form and deep shadows. Just observe all these things and more, without creating images of what is observed, so that the mind is everlastingly new, fresh, innocent and young.

SW: *I have heard it said that you lost most of your*

memory when in the 1920s you experienced that great spiritual illumination.

K : 'Psychological memory' totally dropped off.

SW: *What about 'factual memory'?*

K : Much of my past was also forgotten. I did not forget everything though because I still remembered how to count and how to use words correctly.

SW: *Would you describe your great experience as a form of amnesia, if I may use a medical term?*

K : No. I do not know what causes amnesia. I do not know whether amnesia is caused by brain damage. Don't call it amnesia because what happened was not amnesia. Some called it the awakening of kundalini and all that stuff. The Theosophical leaders were confused and they offered all kinds of explanations at that time. Memory is stored in the brain cells. When the mind is fully transformed the very brain cells experience a mutation.. It is a fundamental change which cannot be explained in scientific terms. Unless you have personally experienced this mutation you will not know what I am talking about.

What is Clairvoyance?

SW: *Please pardon me for wanting to ask you a question on a subject that is bordering on the occult. Often I have seen you brush aside questions concerning occult powers.*

K : Let us talk together as two friends without any barriers between ourselves. What is your question?

SW: *I have read C.W. Leadbeater's remarkable book titled 'Clairvoyance'. Do you know this work?*

K : I know about its existence but I haven't read it. I am not familiar with Theosophical literature. Philosophical, religious and spiritual books bore me and I don't read them.

SW: *Rightly or wrongly such books fascinate me. Krishnaji, you do not have to read them because you are a lucky fount of wisdom but I have to read them because I am a poor unlucky ignoramus.*

K : What is your question?

SW: *Clairvoyance means 'seeing clearly' but it also refers to the ability to see what is hidden from ordinary physical sight. Some people have the capacity to know without using any of their sense organs. On several occasions I have had experiences of a clairvoyant nature. For instance, I recently visited your parental home. I was curiously wanting to see the sacred puja room in which you were born. Some friends kindly took me to your former home in Madanapalle. I was walking ahead of them in this little town. Although I had never even seen a photograph of your home, I unmistakeably identified it the moment I saw it. Besides, I knew all the details of the house's interior even before entering it. The whole house was strangely familiar. In a trance I walked up the stairs and searched for a religious picture in a room. Much to my regret the picture was missing for it had been removed. But the occupant of the house confirmed that I had* *correctly indicated the exact spot on the wall where the picture had once been hanging.*

K : Many people have experiences of that kind. Are you suggesting that you have had an extraordinary mysterious experience?

SW: *In a sense it was a very unusual experience.*

K : Why do you attach importance to this experience or any experience? The experience is over but you are holding onto it.

SW: *What is wrong in treasuring a marvellous experience?*

K : Every experience that is retained burdens the mind and prevents clarity.

SW: *Is experience like a thick mist that clouds the mind?*

K : Exactly.

SW: *I am aware that the attachment to experiences obstructs one's receptivity to further experiences, even so I like to know whether the faculty of clairvoyance operates within the field of the mind or outside it. Shall we examine this matter?*

K : We shall do so presently. Sir, you may or may not have clairvoyant powers. I do not know and I am not interested in the least in finding that out. What is really important is not whether you are clairvoyant but whether you have an image of yourself as a superhuman person with clairvoyant powers. Don't you have such an image of yourself? Why do you have *any* type of image?

SW: *I am keen to know whether clairvoyance operates within the field of the thought process.*

K : One is naturally suspicious about anything that is the product of thought.

SW: *Are you implying that clairvoyance is unreliable, if it is acting within the field of consciousness?*

K : Everything that springs from within consciousness is the known. Therefore our consciousness can never touch the unknown. Let us find out whether clairvoyance is beyond the limitations of thought. Are you seriously interested in this question?

SW: *Indeed I am.*

K : Always be sceptical of persons who claim to have clairvoyance. It is not that clairvoyance does not exist. It certainly exists. But doesn't it feed your vanity to believe that you have gifts lacking in others? A guru once visited me. He tried very hard to impress me. One of the things he told me was that he had clairvoyantly diagnosed that I suffer from hay fever. It is true that I suffer from hay fever. What was the secret of this guru's clairvoyance? Before visiting me, this guru had met a friend of mine and secretly gathered from him this bit of information concerning hay fever! Today this guru cleverly passes himself off as a clairvoyant.

SW: *Krishnaji, on two occasions I noticed that you have clairvoyant powers. At a discussion meeting you criticized the audience for failing to listen carefully. I was seated behind a pillar with the result that you did not notice my presence there. On that occasion I was not able to concentrate on the discussion because I had a painful cramp in the leg. Then I said to myself: 'If K is clairvoyant he will surely* *excuse me for not being attentive'. After the meeting I was surprised when you walked up to me and said: 'Is your leg all right?'*

K : Sometimes I make statements without knowing that I am making them. Some other source seems to be expressing messages through me.

SW: *When I met you at Vasanta Vihar in Madras after flying from Australia, you greeted me and exclaimed: "I know what's in your bag! You are bringing me cheese and an Agatha Christie thriller." You were perfectly right on that occasion because those were exactly the articles in my bag.*

K : Probably it was a shrewd guess that turned out to be right.

SW: *Please explain what is genuine clairvoyance.*

K : A mind that is imageless, without thought, unconditioned, is capable of great clarity. That clarity, which is timeless, cân delve into the future. The future can be foretold. When the mind is free, that clarity will manifest itself even during sleep. That clarity may be called clairvoyance. But the name you give it is unimportant because the name is never the thing itself.

The Mystery of Death

K : Why are you looking so miserable? Why are you so unhappy? What is troubling you? And why have you visited me again?

SW: *Last week a friend of mine died of cancer. It was an agonizing death. The pain he experienced was unbearable. So the doctors drugged him to kill the pain. Therefore he was* *semiconscious during the last days of his life.*

K : What kind of cancer was it?

SW: *It was lung cancer. I have been reflecting that our lives may also have to end some day.*

K : It is not that life *may* end: life *will* end. Sooner or later we will all die.

SW: *Owing to the tremendous advances in medicine, it is not impossible that man may overcome death in the distant future. We have hitherto assumed that we are all mortal. The statement 'man is mortal' is based on our past experience but in the future we may achieve physical immortality.*

K : Such speculations surely originate from the fear of death. If you were not afraid of death you would not be saying these things.

SW: *Are you suggesting that theories concerning reincarnation and the afterlife are the outcome of the fear of death?*

K : The man or woman who lives intensely in the present, the timeless now, will not be interested in the tomorrow. The tomorrow becomes important when you are avoiding what is happening in the present. The old people look to the past and the young look forward to the future. But the person who is living from moment to moment, in the eternal present, will have neither the time nor the inclination to be distracted by thoughts about the past or the future.

SW: *Religious books are replete with theories about what lies in store for us after death. But you are hinting that all these theories are without substance. You are implying that man* *invented these theories because he feared old age and death. I realize that such theories probably came into existence because they fulfilled a certain psychological need. The belief in the possibility of an afterlife considerably reduces our fear of death.*

K : It is a comforting thought that you would be meeting your dead grandmother again in heaven or elsewhere. When your loved ones die, you won't experience pangs of separation because you will feel secure in the knowledge that someday you will be reunited with them.

SW: *After divesting the theory of reincarnation of its psychological origins, shall we reexamine it? Let us temporarily forget the psychological reasons why this theory has such a hold on people and then consider it.*

K : Sir, that is the wrong approach. When you know the psychological background to a belief, when you see that a particular belief was invented by a frightened mind, then won't you throw away that belief? Sir, why have *any* belief? Can't you live *without* beliefs? A sane mind does not need the support of beliefs.

SW: *If the doctors inform me that I am suffering from an incurable illness and that I have only a few days left to live, is it right to request them that I should be put to death painlessly? Do you recommend euthanasia? What is the purpose of prolonging my life by artificial means if I have been reduced to the state of a vegetable as a result of an accident?*

K : Human beings may like to regard themselves as being very clever and marvellous but the truth is that we are still barbarians. Man is violent. That is a fact. He gives expression to that violence by using an unkind word or by torturing someone whom he hates. Killing is an extreme expression of that violence. Whether you get someone else to do the killing or whether you do the dirty work yourself, it still involves the destruction of life. I do not advocate the killing of others, even when it is done painlessly, nor do I support the killing of oneself. Suicide is a manifestation of violence that is directed against oneself.

SW: *Why are we violent?*

K : We are violent because we are selfish. The ruthless pursuit of self-interest is violence. The self is insatiable. The desires and pursuits of the self are endless. The self can only behave selfishly, which is another way of saying that the self can only behave violently.

SW: *I vividly remember how you responded to an overseas telegram you received when we were living in Colombo. A friend of yours telegraphed a message that she was dying. You then sent her a telegram conveying your love with the words 'I AM THINKING OF YOU'.*

K : If you sincerely desire to help a person then you must act during that person's lifetime. Having grand funerals or memorials are meaningless gestures of affection. It is quite hypocritical to pour scorn on an opponent during his lifetime and then pay tributes after the poor fellow is dead.

SW: *Why does one cry one's heart out when a close friend dies?*

K : When a loved person dies it is normal for grief-stricken relatives and friends to cry. Do you cry out of concern for the dead person? Don't you cry because you are suddenly conscious of your own personal loss? The dead person is gone forever and you are faced with a terrible loneliness, an aching emptiness, which can never be filled. And you cry because it gives you some feeling of relief. But no amount of crying or praying will resurrect the dead.

SW: *I suppose it is the absolute finality of death that makes it such a dreadful experience.*

K : When death knocks at your door you cannot say "Please Mr. Death kindly wait for one more week until I have finished my work". When death comes you have to abandon everything and go. You cannot take away your furniture with you. When death comes you will lose all your possessions. You will be permanently separated from your family and friends. It will be the end of all your achievements, your glories, your likes and dislikes. You go away as empty-handed as when you were born.

SW: *You have just said that at the time of death one is compelled to abandon everything and go. May I ask an obvious question? Where do the dead go?*

K : Sir, what are you? You have a name and a bank account, which makes you feel that you are an individual. But do you really exist as a distinct separate person? What are you but a collection of thoughts, emotions, tendencies, predilections, hates, sorrows, fears, ambitions, desires, beliefs and ideas? This combination of qualities is what you are. You are nothing but these qualities. If these qualities were removed, one by one, then what is left? Nothing is left. Therefore there is no such thing as 'yourself' or 'myself'. Do you realize that none of your characteristics is fixed or permanent? Everything in that aggregation, including every thought and feeling, is subject to change. You may like to think that there is hidden somewhere within you an unchangeable substance called a soul. But you will find that 'soul' or 'atman' is only a concept, a creation of the mind as a result of its desire for permanency and security, and like all concepts, this concept is also changeable. When you thus see that there is nothing in you that permanently exists and that the world within and the world without is always in motion, then one is in a position to explore into this question of reincarnation. Everything within your consciousness, including your body, is perpetually changing for the thought process consists of a chain of thoughts in a state of flux. And is your body any different from your mind? Thoughts are dying and being reborn. The body is also dying and being reborn all the time. Is it clear that nothing permanently exists? If nothing permanently exists, then nothing reincarnates. Do you understand the question? Reincarnation becomes a possibility only if there is a permanent unchangeable entity, which alone would be capable of moving from one life to another life, like a passenger who travels from one railway station to another railway station. But if no such passenger exists, if no such entity exists, then surely there is nothing to reincarnate. Reincarnation is only a theory born of man's desire for continuity.

SW: *I am quite familiar with your writings on the all-important subject of death. You have stated that psychological death should precede bodily death.*

K : That is correct. Can the 'you' die before you die?

SW: *Before the occurrence of physical death, I hope I would die to all my likes, dislikes, worries, fears and so forth. How nice if I were capable of dying to my entire past!*

K : Once you have died to your entire past you will discover a new beginning.

SW: *Is that all?*

K : When the mind has been cleansed of the past, when it is free of time, one will come upon something that is indestructible.

SW: *Are you ready to discard your body?*

K : When the time comes for me to go, I will walk into the house of death with a smile.

What is Sanity?

SW: *Yesterday I called on a person who is undergoing treatment in a mental hospital. Meeting so many demented men and women there was a most depressing experience. Have you ever tried to help an inmate of a mental hospital?*

K : On one occasion I visited a lunatic asylum to see a patient whom I happened to know. Then

I realized that the 'insane' who lived inside the lunatic asylum were not fundamentally different from the 'sane' who lived outside it!

SW: *I have heard it said that a thin border divides the insane from the sane.*

K : That's not the point. Perhaps there is no such border. Have the so-called sane more clarity than the so-called insane? In mental hospitals you will meet men who seriously believe that they are kings or dictators and women who believe that they are queens or princesses. A person is regarded as being insane when he believes in things that have no connection with reality. Is it not sheer insanity to believe in the existence of fanciful gods — imaginary gods with many hands and heads?

SW: *Indian philosophers have regarded the act of mistaking a rope for a snake as an instance of distorted perception.*

K : Our perception at present is covered with a veil of images. We have images about the people we meet. Parents have images about their children and children have images about their parents. Many people who attend my talks have a certain image about me. It is unfortunate that I have a reputation of being a spiritual teacher. Therefore they read more into my words than what was intended. So they misunderstand the simple obvious truths I talk about. This image about me prevents the right understanding of my talks. A sane mind has no images.

SW: *Is retaining images a sign of insanity?*

K : Of course it is.

SW: *Aren't there degrees of insanity?*

K : There is no qualitative difference between a mind that has few images and one with many. Haven't you noticed how even a single prejudice makes the mind crooked? The image that persons belonging to a particular race or religion are of inferior quality and evil-minded produces feelings of hatred for them. Hatred eventually results in intolerance, terrorism and war. The images we have about others may not correspond with what they actually are. These images are a far cry from reality. But we get attached to our images and that is one of our difficulties.

SW: *Do you think that psychoanalysis is helpful for certain mental disorders?*

K : Have the psychoanalysts themselves freed their minds of images? If they have not done so, would they not be imposing their own particular brand of images on their poor patients? Psychoanalysts may succeed in making patients disciplined well-behaved members of society. But psychoanalysts should question the very foundations of society. What is the good of making patients conform to the rules of society so that they become respectable citizens? The very core of society is corrupt. Is not society based on competition, ambition and selfishness? And who is the 'analyser' who does the analysis? Is the 'analyser' any different from what is analysed? The 'analyser' is the product of the mind's confusion. Whatever the 'analyser' does must therefore result in further confusion. As I have often said, analysis is paralysis. Why depend on anyone to probe into yourself? Must you not be a light unto yourself? A person who constantly explores the mind, who is ever watchful of its movements and self-reliant, wouldn't touch a psychoanalyst with a barge pole.

I must tell you a story. An inmate of a mental hospital loved to spend hours trying to fish for trout in his cup of coffee. He used a cigarette as a fishhook. An amused psychoanalyst questioned the patient: "Sir, have you caught many fish today?"

The patient replied: "Are you crazy? Can't you see that this is only a cup of coffee?"

Energy for Self-examination

SW: *I have been counselling a colleague with a sexual problem. He wants me to discuss his problem with you.*

K : Why hasn't he accompanied you today?

SW: *He is reluctant to meet you because he feels that he would be nervous in your company.*

K : I won't bite him! Tell him that he is welcome here. What is troubling him?

SW: *He is trying to overcome his homosexuality.*

K : Sir, the word 'homosexuality' is rather derogatory. Can't you avoid using that word?

SW: *But it is a neutral scientific word.*

K : That may be so but today many people have a condemnatory attitude towards homosexuality. The very fact that he wishes to overcome his homosexuality shows that he is already prejudiced against it. I am not saying that homosexuality is desirable or undesirable. If you want to understand any problem you must not condemn it at all. There is no freshness in your way of approaching the problem if you are hostile to it Censorious attitudes prevent one looking at it anew. You have to face the problem exactly as it is, without wanting to alter it in any way. Words have various associations. Words evoke the past; words are the past. Is it possible to look at the problem directly, without seeing it through the screen of words?

SW: *If I shouldn't use the word 'homosexuality', how then shall I refer to it?*

K : Do you have to call it anything?

SW: *Shall I call it X?*

K : Do you realize that the solution to a problem lies in the problem itself? Words will distract your attention from the problem.

SW: *Krishnaji, please lay down guidelines on how to help someone in distress.*

K : I'm afraid there is no method. The art of seeing properly will solve all problems. It is not that you see first and act later because the seeing is itself the doing.

SW: *I've been suggesting to him that he should approach the problem without any sense of condemnation or justification of it.*

K : First of all it is necessary to divest his mind of all sense of sin. He cannot possibly face the problem honestly so long as his mind is tormented by fear or feelings of guilt. When the mind is free of such burdens then it is already intelligent.

SW: *This person is a poet and a novelist. He is highly intelligent and sensitive.*

K : The sexual act is momentary. It is a fleeting experience but why are people so preoccupied with it? Sex is neither pure nor impure but thought magnifies it out of all proportion. Sex is given such inordinate importance by the mind. You either enjoy thinking about a sexual act that is long over or you fantasize about future sexual experiences.

SW: *The mind is the culprit. A wit has remarked that sexuality is not in the genitals but in the mind. Man's obsession with sex is the price he has to pay for having a highly developed imagination.*

K : It is the intellectual people who are troubled by sex. The loving and kind-hearted folk, whose lives are not dominated by the intellect, have hardly turned sex into a problem.

SW: *There is another category of persons who have made sex a problem. I am thinking of the puritanical men and women who have been trained to fight sex as though it were some kind of monster.*

K : I knew a sannyasin in India who struggled with his sexual urge. The more he tried to suppress it the more uncontrollable it became. He did not realize that suppressing his sexual instinct was the surest way of strengthening it. Instead of trying to understand this strong human drive by observing it carefully, he tried very hard to stamp it out but he was unsuccessful. Then rather foolishly he underwent an operation that involved the surgical removal of his sexual organs. He visited me one day and tearfully complained that his body was developing breasts and other female characteristics as a result of this operation.

SW: *The religious traditions of India emphasize the importance of conserving one's energies as a sine qua non for spiritual enlightenment.*

K : Sexual indulgence results in a dissipation of energy. Sexual suppression also results in a dissipation of energy because it reduces the mind to a state of conflict. And conflict, this battle between the powerful desire that wants to indulge in sex and the opposing thought which says 'you must not indulge', brings about a loss of energy. One needs a great deal of energy for self-examination but this energy cannot be accumulated through sexual suppression. There will be an abundance of energy only when the mind is without conflict. When it is understood that the 'I', the entity which had hitherto tried hard to control the movements of thought, is itself the product of thought, then the conflict between the 'thinker' and thought will immediately end. Observe the illusory nature of the 'controller' of thought. All conflict will thereupon end and a new energy will revitalize the mind.

SW: *In certain South Indian temples the linga, the phallus of Lord Shiva, is worshipped. What is the esoteric significance, if any, of linga worship?*

K : Primitive man failed to understand the workings of the procreative instinct. It was a mystery that completely baffled him. He was therefore frightened of it. So he started worshipping it in the same way that he worshipped the elements. What the mind fails to comprehend, it fears. What it fears is either suppressed or worshipped. All forms of worship and prayer originate in fear.

SW: *You once stated that the craving for sexual activity exists because it is a means of self-forgetfulness.*

K : Our lives are centred around the self. Nearly everything we do, think or feel is somehow closely or distantly connected with the self. Sex provides an instant release from the restrictive miserable world of the self. That is why our culture gives such tremendous prominence to sex.

SW: *I suppose a liberated individual would be absolutely free of sex in thought, word and deed.*

K : Such a human being is not troubled by sex nor any psychological problem. When the self ceases to exist of its own accord, then there is bliss.

Awareness is a Game

SW: *After all these many years of self-observation, isn't it shameful that the image-making process still continues in my mind? The torrential rain of thought never stops pouring down. One feels depressed in defeat.*

K : Why do you judge yourself? As a child you must have played games. Awareness is also like a game. If you play only for the fun of it, does it matter whether you win or lose?

SW: *I find that awareness is not continuous. There are flashes of awareness. The flashes stop and then there are moments of dullness. One is suddenly aware again. This intermittent nature of awareness is a problem.*

K : Awareness does not have to be continuous: seldom is it continuous. When you criticize yourself by saying that awareness is not continuous, it shows that you have formed a concept of awareness, an ideal, a standard. Thereafter you try to conform to that standard established by yourself. Sir, awareness is not a self-imposed practice. You cannot practise awareness. When you have an insight into the way your mind works, do not become greedy for more insights by saying the mind should be aware all the time'.

SW: *I feel fatigued after trying to be aware from moment to moment.*

K : Take a rest when you are tired. After you have refreshed yourself, then you are ready for work again. Self-observation involves very hard work. Without energy you cannot work and when energy has depleted by work then you have to rest again.

SW: *I seem to expend more energy when the mind is struggling to be alert.*

K : Struggling to be alert is a waste of energy whereas *being* alert generates energy. Have you noticed that there is actually an increased energy when you come to terms with yourself? Let us consider fear. The mind loves to escape from fear by justifying its existence or brushing it aside. You do not eliminate fear by escaping from it. But the moment the fact of fear is accepted and fully faced, without running away from it, fear disappears and a new energy comes into being.

SW: *The memories of certain pleasant and unpleasant experiences often recur. Certain thoughts are so deeply entangled in consciousness that they seem to be permanently residing there.*

K : Whenever a thought recurs you must look at it anew. An annoying thought or a pleasurable thought that keeps on emerging has a story to tell. Why not allow the fellow to reveal his own story? Can't you find out a little more about the fellow each time he emerges?

SW: *My other difficulty is the rapidity of the thought process. It moves so fast that I cannot keep pace with it.*

K : It will calm down as you uncover the layers of the unconscious. You must lay bare the unconscious so that there are no dark corners within it.

SW: *I experience periods of tranquility, when thought has temporarily fallen into abeyance. It is a pity that these periods are not of longer duration.*

K : Why ask for more? Surely it is thought that is demanding tranquility. There will certainly be no tranquility so long as thought operates. On one occasion a very learned friend remarked that he had read a great deal with the result that there was no space in his mind. Can a mind that is very active and full of its own noise ever have the silence to receive something untouched by thought? Sir, if I may suggest, try to be alone for at least one hour every day. During this period you should not read, work or enjoy the company of your friends. You may devote this time for taking a solitary walk or observing nature. It is a sheer delight to watch the birds in flight, the lovely green trees and the vast open skies. The mind loses its sensitivity whenever there is no communion with nature. Live close to nature.

SW: *Is it necessary to know every thought?*

K : You cannot possibly know every thought. There are far too many of them. The stream of consciousness is enormous and powerful. Only by understanding the limitations of thought can you transcend it. The very act of understanding is also the act of crossing this stream. You have got to walk out of it. Sir, walk out of it right now!

The Enigma that was J. Krishnamurti

Being in a permanent and continuous state of samadhi is the traditionally accepted hallmark of Self-realised persons. Their samadhi is always continuous; it is never occasional. It is not experienced intermittently.

Variously described as "the otherness", "the intensity" or "the immensity" in Krishnamurti's writings, his samadhi came to him by fits and starts. All the evidence points towards the fact that his states of samadhi were short-lived:

"Very early this morning, many hours before dawn, on waking there was that piercing intensity of strength with its sternness. There was in this sternness, bliss. By the watch it 'lasted' for forty-five minutes with increasing intensity. The stream and the quiet night, with their brilliant stars, were within it.[1]

"Every thought, every feeling was gone and the brain was utterly still. . . And of a sudden that unknowable

---

Originally published in *The Mountain Path,* vol. 28, Nos. 1 & 2, June 1991 immensity was there, not only in the room and beyond but also deep, in the innermost recesses, which was once the mind."[2]

During those periods when K was not overpowered by "the otherness" he behaved like an ordinary human being in the sense that he was subject to states of fear, anxiety, shyness, irritability and depression. Yet he was an exceptional person because he was almost devoid of envy, hate or violence.

Before giving public talks K used to feel shy and nervous. But when swayed by "the otherness" his personality changed noticeably, especially in the act of delivering a discourse. His diffidence temporarily disappeared and he always spoke like a man under the influence of an unseen power. Then he would seem to be in a trance and words of wisdom flowed from his lips. Often, after a discourse, he had no recollection of what he had just been saying. Immediately after fulfilling his special mission as a spiritual teacher, K would revert to the psychological state of an ordinary human being. It is a pity that K's biographers have overlooked the fact that he had this dual personality. They have failed to understand that most of the time K behaved like any ordinary mortal and a very lovable one at that; but at other times, he became a human channel for the manifestation of the divine "otherness".

Do Self-realised persons experience the state of being united with Brahman only temporarily or permanently? Ramana Maharshi remarked that "a person who has been going about in the sun feels cool when he reaches the shade. Someone who keeps on going from the shade into the sun and then back into the shade is a fool. A wise man stays permanently in the shade. Similarly, the mind of the one who knows the truth does not leave Brahman. The mind of the ignorant, on the contrary, revolves in the world, feeling miserable, and for a little time returns to Brahman to experience happiness. In fact, what is called the world is only thought. When the world disappears, i.e. when there is no thought, the mind experiences happiness; and when the world appears, it goes through misery."[3]

Thought, according to K, cannot heal any psychological wounds because thought is itself the wound. Thought cannot liberate us because thought is itself the main obstacle to Liberation. K said: "Is not Reality ever the uncreated? And must not the mind cease to create, to formulate, if it would experience the Uncreated?"[4] Reality, then, is to be found in the interval between two thoughts. So long as man remains enslaved to thought, and conditioned by thought, he can never find that indescribable, unconditioned state of bliss. The mind is incapable of transcending its own frontiers. Hence, however hard the mind tries to improve itself through various kinds of disciplines, practices and sadhanas, such actions will be of no avail. Yet, K contradicted himself by insisting that unless spiritual aspirants work *very hard* they will never succeed in discovering the Absolute. Now, is it really possible to work without exercising the mind at all? Any resort to effort necessarily involves the use of the conditioned mind. K distrusted thought to such an extent that he urged us never to use it for a spiritual purpose: "You may not invite Reality, it must come to you; you may not choose Reality, it must choose you."[5] After having likened Reality to a kind of grace, he still wanted us to work hard. The problem is that the moment I involve myself in any activity that is directed towards my spiritual upliftment I have found that I invariably activate the thought process.

Ramana's teachings are devoid of confusion as regards this question of thought. While fully recognising the limitations of thought, he pointed out a helpful and practical method of *using* thought to bring about its own demise. When Ramana was asked how the mind will become quiescent, he replied: "By the inquiry 'Who am I?'. The thought 'who am I?' will destroy all other thoughts, and, like the stick used for stirring the burning pyre, it will itself in the end get destroyed. Then, there will arise Self-realization. . . When other thoughts arise, one should not pursue them, but should inquire: 'To whom did they arise?' It does not matter how many thoughts arise. As each thought arises, one should inquire with diligence, "To whom has this thought arisen?'. The answer that would emerge would be 'To me'. Thereupon if one inquires 'Who am I?', the mind will go back to its source; and the thought that arose will become quiescent. With repeated practice in this manner, the mind will develop the skill to stay in its source."[6]

K and Ramana differed widely on the question of the usefulness of thought as a means of attaining union with the Absolute. According to K the mind can never think accurately about God. Such thinking can only result in the formation of mere opinions and beliefs that have no relationship whatsoever to the actuality of God. Why be satisfied with a concept of God that is only a fictitious creation of the imagination? But Ramana taught that thinking of the Self is not without value: "He who gives himself up to the Self that is God is the most excellent devotee. Giving one's self up to God means remaining constantly in the Self without giving room for the rise of any thoughts other than the thought of the Self."[7]

One is heartened by the fact that Ramana did not view thought in black and white terms. Like nuclear energy, thought can be immensely destructive if wrongly used but equally it is capable of elevating us to the very threshold of divinity.

K urged his listeners to be constantly aware of their thoughts and feelings without in any way condemning or justifying them. The wandering of the mind can be ended by thinking through and feeling to the end *every* thought-feeling. Such awareness involves the avoidance of judging or evaluating one's stream of consciousness. During the 1940s he advocated an effortless and passive awareness. Many persons who experimented on this themselves complained that such a method was not only arduous but failed to liberate them. Then in 1956 K contradicted himself: he stated that total awareness cannot be maintained all the time. He therefore suggested a minute or two of total awareness followed by a period of relaxation, during which one can observe the operations of one's mind. Awareness is central to K's teachings. Although he insisted upon awareness as the means of transcending the limitations of the mind and arriving at the discovery of Truth (despite his contradictory dictum that 'Truth is a pathless land'[8]), it is doubtful if any of his listeners actually found Liberation. The countless thousands in various countries who listened to K got nowhere. By observing their thought processes for years they found that they were becoming increasingly enmeshed in thought. Instead of their minds becoming dissolved, they realised to their dismay that they were becoming more and more cerebral.

K maintained that it is thought that creates the thinker. The 'I' is merely a fictitious invention of thought. Hence the dissolution of thought automatically results in the dissolution of the 'I'. K's teaching in this regard was diametrically opposed to that of Ramana who said: "Of all the thoughts that arise in the mind, the 'I' thought is the first. It is only after the rise of this that the other thoughts arise."[9]

Much more important than the question of the origin of thought is that of its ending. K refused to prescribe any methods or techniques for this purpose. He said that thought will end of and by itself when there is full understanding of the thought process. Presumably, this faculty of understanding comes into being when the mind is free of thought. Is it any help to be told that one comes by this no-thought state, and that it occurs accidentally, without any exertion of effort?

I was closely associated with K and his worldwide activities for more than three decades. His human and endearing qualities as well as his siddhis have been described in my work *J. Krishnamurti as I knew him*[10]. Although his mind was extraordinarily clear and profound, one is puzzled by the fact that K was also a confusing bundle of contradictions. The task of reconciling the different sides of his enigmatic personality is not easy. It is for the reader to discover, if possible, any elements of unity and harmony that may underlie the contradictions listed below.

In the Asian world it is generally the case that the lives of saints are characterised by a certain simplicity and austerity. Although K advocated simple living, he actually led a life of luxury amidst the rich and famous. He was always the darling and protégé of the wealthy and privileged. K wore beautifully tailored suits and only handmade shoes pleased him. What a contrast to Ramana and all the other sages of his lineage who were content with a mere loincloth! He also enjoyed travelling in high-powered motor cars. Indeed his passion for cars was legendary. Surrounded though he was by material possessions, it is significant that he was indifferent to them. He was somehow not attached to the things of this world and was always ready to give away any of his belongings to those in need.

With all the rhetoric that he could muster, K denounced the activities of *all* gurus whom he likened to exploiters of the gullible. He insisted on absolute self-reliance in spiritual matters. Those who are confused, acting out of their own confusion, cannot but select gurus who are also confused. The clear-sighted need no gurus, he argued, because they are lights unto themselves. That may be so but how many have that rare clarity which characterises the enlightened? By denouncing all gurus was he not doing an injustice to that minority of Self-realised gurus who are really genuine? By casting aspersions on other teachers was he not subtly promoting his own teachings? Although he severely criticised the institution of the guru, was he not himself, to all intents and purposes, a kind of guru? K did not of course have a beard and wear saffron coloured clothes but he was the spiritual instructor to thousands of his admirers. Like any other guru, K counselled numerous persons who had psychological problems. To the distressed he privately prescribed sadhanas despite his publicly declared opposition to all spiritual practices.

K rebuked photographers who tried to take pictures of his radiant face. But he did not mind being photographed by specially selected persons. Towards the end of his life there was even an official photographer! He tried to create the impression that he disapproved the glorification of his personality. Yet he permitted the use of his name for the establishment of various foundations, information centres and schools. He soon became the expositor of a body of teachings which had given rise to a cult. The followers of K resent the word 'guru' but is he not a respected father figure to them?

All ashrams were held in abomination by K. He stated that meditation, which is a voyage of self-discovery, should be done individually and never within the restrictive presence of a body of persons. So he described group meditation as a 'vulgarity'. He regarded ashrams as 'concentration camps' where the mind is subjected to conditioning influences. Nevertheless, K was responsible for initiating several educational centres where students and teachers are expected to devote much time to self-observation while living communally. During his lifetime K regularly guided his followers at these centres which are really ashrams in essence.

Organised religions and other spiritual organisations were vehemently condemned by K. So in 1929, after 18 years of its existence, K dissolved his own Order of the Star. It was a bold act that resulted in thousands of his disciples feeling lost and leaderless. After declaring that "my only concern is to set men absolutely, unconditionally free"[11], why did he later in life (in the 1960s) establish several Krishnamurti Foundations in the world? What he did was clearly inconsistent with his earlier opposition to such organisations. Many of his friends were disillusioned with him. There were some who kept away from his talks as a token of protest. K's reputation for integrity was severely shattered and the situation worsened when some of the trustees of his organisations started misusing their powers. Vast sums of money were collected in his name and at the time of his death in 1986 these wealthy organisations were rife with intrigues and power struggles. What had originally been a pure teaching, with its emphasis on self-reliance and self-observation with a view to the purification of the mind, was sadly vitiated by the lure of gold and real estate. That was the unfortunate aspect of K's legacy.

The only explanation for K's strange behaviour is that he was easily influenced by those around him. His mind was so malleable that it was easily bent by unscrupulous people to their advantage. It was this quality of innocent openness that helped to make him a superb medium. We shall return to this theme later in this essay.

When Bishop Leadbeater discovered the boy K, the Theosophists were quick to recognise the youngster's vacant mind, with its enormous spiritual potential. He had a certain vagueness and openness and all the makings of a marvellous medium. So they declared that K was destined to be the 'Vehicle of the World Teacher'. It is to be noted that K was going to be only the chosen vehicle, the medium or spokesman of the Lord Maitreya, the future Buddha, and *not* the great Teacher himself. Like the Prophet Mohammed, his role was that of a mere messenger. Messengers of God have to be faithful reporters of the sacred word but do *not necessarily* have to be divine themselves.

When K was asked whether he was in fact the World Teacher, he evaded the question by saying that it is the teachings that are important and not the label or designation given to the person who expresses them. What matters is the song and not the name of the singer. However K never denied his special destiny. He was deeply conscious of his extraordinary mission in life despite his repeated denials of having any image of himself.

Was K just an ordinary human being most of the time, who sometimes gave expression to divine messages? If we accept this possibility, as certain Theosophists do, it helps considerably to understand K's dual nature. It explains his many contradictions.

No account of K is complete without a reference to his great compassion for all beings. He loved all equally but he seemed to have favourites. He was seriously concerned about the problem of human suffering and sincerely felt that it was his personal responsibility to alleviate it. His boundless love even extended to the wild animals he met in the course of his solitary walks in jungles and other places. He had no fear of dangerous animals and in this respect he was like Ramana. Buddhists believe that compassion will be the predominant feature of the future Maitreya Buddha. It is indeed significant that K was an embodiment of loving kindness; it is also noteworthy that his teachings have a Buddhist flavour. Was he then a harbinger of the future Enlightened One?

As a young man K composed mystical poems. What follows is an excerpt from one of his poetical works entitled *The Immortal Friend*[12] wherein K describes a vision he had — a vision of the Buddha.

> I sat a-dreaming in a room of great silence.
> The early morning was still and breathless,
> The great blue mountains stood against the dark skies, cold and clear,
> Round the dark log house

The black and yellow birds were welcoming the
sun.

I sat on the floor, with legs crossed, meditating,
Forgetting the sunlit mountains,
The birds,
The immense silence,
And the golden sun.

I lost the feel of my body,
My limbs were motionless,
Relaxed and at peace.
A great joy of unfathomable depth filled my heart.
Eager and keen was my mind, concentrated.
Lost to the transient world,
I was full of strength.

As the Eastern breeze
That suddenly springs into being
And calms the weary world,
There in front of me
Seated cross-legged,
As the world knows Him
In His yellow robes, simple and magnificent,
Was the Teacher of Teachers.

Looking at me,
Motionless the Mighty Being sat.
I looked and bowed my head,
My body bent forward of itself.

That one look
Showed the progress of the world,
Showed the immense distance between the world
And the greatest of its Teachers.
How little it understood,
And how much He gave.
How joyously He soared,
Escaping from birth and death,
From its tyranny and entangling wheel.

Elightenment attained,
He gave to the world, as the flower gives
Its scent,
The Truth.

As I looked
At the sacred feet that once trod the happy
Dust of India,
My heart poured forth its devotion,
Limitless and unfathomable,
Without restraint and without effort.

That K had certain shortcomings was a matter of considerable sadness to the countless thousands who adored him. Was he inwardly a fully transformed spiritual master,.despite all the imperfections that were evident in his outward behaviour? Who am I to judge? Perhaps it is best to ignore his personality, forget the man K who is no more, and concentrate instead on the marvellous spiritual teachings that were given to the world through him.

References

1. J. Krishnamurti — *Krishnamurti's Notebook,* London: Victor Gollancz, 1976, p. 81
2. *Ibid.* p.251-252
3. Ramana Maharshi — *Who am I*? 10th edition, Tiruvannamalai: T.N. Venkataraman, 1966, p.11
4. J. Krishnamurti — *Authentic Report of Sixteen Talks* given in *1945 & 1946,* Ojai: Krishnamurti Writings, 1947, p. 26
5. *Ibid.* p. 38
6. Ramana Maharshi — *Who am I*? p. 4
7. *Ibid.* p. 8
8. J. Krishnamurti — *The Dissolution of the Order of the Star,* Ommen: Star Publishing Trust, 1929, p.3
9. Ramana Maharshi — *Who am I*? p. 4
10. Susunaga Weeraperuma — *J. Krishnamurti as I Knew Him,* Bombay: Chetana, 1988
11. J. Krishnamurti — *The Dissolution of the Order of the Star,* p. 14
12. J. Krishnamurti — *The Immortal Friend,* Ommen: Star Publishing Trust, 1928, p. 8-10